you and me
FOREVER

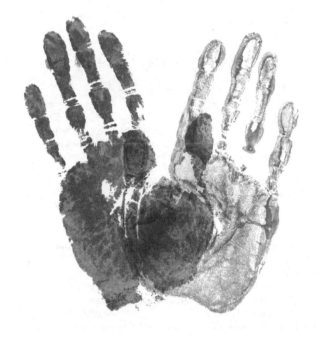

marriage in light of eternity

FRANCIS CHAN & LISA CHAN

You and me FOREVER

Published by Claire Love Publishing
4100 3rd Street / San Francisco, CA 94124

Hardcover ISBN: 978-0-9903514-1-2
Paperback ISBN: 978-0-9903514-0-5
eBook ISBN: 978-0-9903514-2-9

Cover Design: Dann Petty
Hand Lettering: Jim Elliston
Typeset: Peter Gloege
Author Photo: Tamiz Photography

Printed in the United States of America
21 20 19 18 17 16 15 14 (DP) 10 9 8 7 6 5 4 3 2 1

To Rachel, Mercy, Eliana, Ezekiel, and Claire.
The greatest kids we could ever ask for.
Thanks to Jesus, we get to be with you forever.

CONTENTS

ACKNOWLEDGMENTS

This project was total a team effort. Literally thousands of hours went into this project by filmmakers, editors, production crews, actors, web developers, app developers, marketers, designers, and musicians.

A special thanks to those who believed in this message so much that you volunteered your time and services. We believe that great rewards await.

It was a blast working with such a ridiculously gifted team!

Kevin Kim—Thanks for coordinating this whole project from start to finish. We wouldn't have even tried to pull this off without your leadership. You're a stud.

Liz Matthews—You are a freak of nature. Assistant, accountant, babysitter…you've done it all and have become family to us. And you put up with Kevin the slave driver. We love you.

Julie Chow—Thanks for paying attention to every detail of self publishing. You're amazing. I'm going to misspell sum words hear just too bug you.

Shawn Gordon, Tony Mattero, Nate Hanson, Alejandro Cortes, Marcus Bailey, Billy Wark, Kevin Sheddon, Atoo Sakhrani, Marcus Hung—Thank you for being great pastors, loving the people, sharing the work.

All the boys at Project Bayview. We love you and can't believe how much God has changed your lives.

Jessica Henry—Thanks for your encouragement and countless hours of work. Thanks for everything you do to help rescue girls around the world.

Dann Petty—Thanks for designing the cover and putting up with a dozen amateurs throwing in our two cents every other day.

Matthew Ridenour and the marketing team.

Chris Chiu, Chris Lee, Zach Johnston, Eyuel Tessema, Nati Tessema, Josh Pritchard and the rest of the tech team that helped make an amazing app and e-book.

Thank you to all the incredible filmmakers who helped spread the message by creating short films that inspired us toward greater marriages.

Thank you to all the advocates of this project who spread the word, pushing the book out as far and wide as possible.

INTRODUCTION

The Secret to Happily Ever After

I love Lisa Chan. There is no human being I love more. We fell madly in love with each other and were married in 1994. Twenty years and five kids later, the love keeps growing. Day after day, she has stood faithfully by my side—loving me, encouraging me, and challenging me. She is my best friend. Life together has been amazing. And the best is yet to come. I'm sure of it.

Even now, I am working to make sure that my family is set up for the future. When most people make that statement, they are talking about financial security for their last few years on earth. When I say it, I'm referring to the millions of years that come after that. People accuse me of going overboard in preparing for my first ten million years in eternity. In my opinion, people go overboard in worrying about their last ten years on earth.

I have imagined what it will be like when Lisa comes face to face with God. The Bible guarantees this will actually happen. One day, my wife will stand before the Creator and Judge of all things. What a staggering moment that will be! I can't imagine any of us being ready for the shock of that day, yet Scripture begs us to spend our lives preparing for it.

I'm not suggesting that we work to earn God's acceptance. That would be heresy. We are welcomed into His presence if we trust in what Jesus did on the cross (John 3:16, Eph. 2:1–9, 2 Cor. 5:21). It's His work—not ours—that determines our eternal fate. The Bible could not be more clear that good works do not earn us a spot in the Kingdom; living and active faith in Jesus does. Followers of Christ can look forward to that final day with great security—even anticipation (2 Pet. 3:11–12). Nonetheless, the Bible says much about preparing for that day by "working out our salvation" (Philip. 2:12–13).

Because I am crazy about Lisa, I want her to have a great life. But more than that, I want her to have a great eternity. I want her to look back at her life without regret. I want her to be confident that the time she spent on earth prepared her for heaven. Most importantly, I want her to hear God say, "Well done, good and faithful servant. You have been faithful over a little; I will set you over much. Enter into the joy of your master" (Matt. 25:23).

Think of all the awards, promotions, accolades, and accomplishments you would love to receive in your lifetime. Go crazy in imagining it all. And then answer this: Could anything be better than hearing those words from Jesus in the first moments of eternity?

A strange thing happened when Lisa and I started living with an eternal lens: it caused us to enjoy the here and now! Many people will tell you to focus on your marriage, to focus on each other; but we discovered that focusing on God's mission made our marriage amazing. This caused us to experience Jesus deeply—what could be better?

Eternal-mindedness keeps us from silly arguments. There's no time to fight. We have better things to pursue than our interests. Too much is at stake! God created us for a purpose. We can't afford to waste our lives. We can't afford to waste our marriage by merely pursuing our own happiness.

In shepherding a single congregation for 16 years, we had the pleasure of watching couples make radical decisions based on their devotion to Jesus. It was a thrill to see them catch the vision and reap the blessing. We have many sweet memories of enjoying Jesus with these godly couples.

On the flip side, we have grieved as we watched couples pursue happiness while neglecting their mission on earth. We have counseled many who were frustrated because they desired to live biblically but their spouse did not. I can't tell you how many times we agonized for those who were missing out on God's blessing and His intent for marriage. It is partially this sadness that compelled Lisa and I to write this book.

We are sad for the hurting couples; it breaks our hearts, actually. But we are even more brokenhearted about the effect it has on the Kingdom. We are sad because godly marriages magnify God's ingenious creation, but few marriages radiate that glory. We are sad about the victory Satan enjoys in watching couples call themselves "Christian" while living idly, living for themselves. We are devastated by how many choose divorce over obeying the King. The sad state of marriage makes the bride of Christ look dirty and unattractive. We write in hopes of changing some of this.

Recently, we have met many singles who fear marriage. They watched friends who were passionate followers of Christ get married. The result was either an obsession with the pleasures of family or an unending string of arguments and counseling sessions. We are writing to say that it doesn't have to be this way. You can be more effective together than apart. In a truly healthy relationship, we enable each other to accomplish more than we could have done alone. This was His plan.

We are so grateful that God has allowed us to work together on this book. It is an honor for us to brag about our God together. The creation of marriage was a brilliant idea. Our prayer is that we will be able to shed some light on just how beautiful it can be.

But let me warn you. A Christ-centered and eternity-minded marriage is not the same thing as a "fun" marriage. Lisa and I have a blast together, but some of the decisions we make are painful. Yet we know they are right. Christ promises the abundant life (John 10:10), but that is not always synonymous with fun. Some of the truths we share in these pages will lead you to pain. But tough decisions made for God's glory produce a good and right pain, a pain that believers are meant to endure in this fallen world. It's a pain that makes us stronger, holier, more in love with God and each other. Any suffering for His sake is a constant reminder of our future where all the pain will be exchanged for glory.

There are plenty of marriage books that will teach you how to get along and be happy. This is not one of those books. I am not knocking those. In fact, we have learned some helpful principles from them over the years. The problem with those books is that they can make you feel like having a happy family is the goal of Christianity. They can make primary things like God's glory and His mission sound secondary. They can nudge you into exchanging ultimate happiness for immediate happiness. To put it bluntly, those books don't account for the fact that you can have a happy earthly marriage and then be miserable for all eternity. This book is about loving each other forever.

I love my wife. I love marriage. I love *love*. They all point to the brilliance of Jesus, who created them all. I'm guessing you are reading this book because you are either in love or hoping to be. I pray you allow the Holy Spirit to lead you into an eternal love—a love that magnifies Jesus now and forever.

Father, help us love wisely.

MORE THAN A BOOK, HOPEFULLY

Lisa and I hope that this resource will literally change your marriage and possibly your eternity. We have all read books that were good, informative, but not life changing—especially now, when information is more accessible than ever. Many of us keep a steady stream of information flowing into our brains without taking time to meditate and apply what we have already learned. For this reason, we have built in opportunities to **read**, **meditate**, and **act**. We want you to experience God, not just learn about Him.

As you will notice, most of the book is written from my (Francis') voice, even though we came up with many of these ideas together. However, each chapter also contains a section that Lisa wrote on her own. In addition to writing, we also created some videos. Since Lisa and I both feel more comfortable speaking than writing, we made some fun, creative videos where we expressed thoughts that might not have translated well into print. Hopefully, the videos will enhance the lessons that we wrote as well as give you visual glimpses into our family.

For those reading this from the interactive ebook or app, you will notice that the videos are embedded right into the text. For those reading the paper copy of the book, you can find the videos online at www.youandmeforever.org.

MOST IMPORTANTLY...

As you read through the following chapters, you will find that we conclude each chapter with a call to action. This is critical. If you fail to act on what you're learning, this book is doing more harm than good.

> "If I had not come and spoken to them, they would not have been guilty of sin, but now they have no excuse for their sin." (John 15:22)

Christians in America have become experts at conviction—and failures at action. But the first Christians were quick to act. If you remember the day of Pentecost (Acts 2), the people heard Peter's sermon and immediately asked: "What shall we do?" To which Peter answered, "Repent and be baptized." How did they respond? Three thousand of them went straight to the water to be baptized. That's the way it's supposed to happen. As we get convicted by a message, we should be asking, "What should I do in response to this truth?"

We have come up with action points as suggestions, but we don't pretend to know exactly how God is calling you to respond. If you want to know *exactly* what *you* should do, the best answer we can give is: *something!* While we cannot possibly know the next step for you, we can guarantee there is one. The worst thing you can do is nothing.

> But be doers of the word, and *not hearers only*, deceiving yourselves. (James 1:22)

I recently read an article about the fattest people on earth, people weighing well over a thousand pounds, people who are eating themselves to death. At a certain point, they lost the ability to walk. Eventually, they were bedridden and depended on others feeding them because they could no longer even feed themselves.

It reminded me of a lot of people I find in the church. They are fed more and more knowledge every week. They attend church services, join small group Bible studies, read Christian books, listen to podcasts—and are convinced they still need more knowledge. Truth is, their biggest need is to *do something*. They don't need another feast on doctrine. They need to exercise. They need to work off what they've already consumed. Some have become so used to consuming the Word without applying it that you wonder if they even can. These are the spiritually bedridden, resigned to spending the rest of their lives studying the Word without ever making disciples or tangibly caring for others. These are the ones about whom James asks:

> What good is it, my brothers, if someone says he has faith but does not have works? Can that faith save him? (James 2:14)

Sometimes people are paralyzed by fear of failure. They are so afraid that they might do the wrong thing that they do nothing. We need to learn to err on the side of action, because we tend to default to negligence. So many won't do anything unless they hear a voice from heaven telling them precisely what to do. Why not default to action until you hear a voice from heaven telling you to wait? For example: Why not assume you should adopt kids unless you hear a voice telling you not to? Wouldn't that seem more biblical since God has told us that true religion is to care for the widows and orphans (James 1:27)?

One reason we don't err on the side of action is the harsh criticism we receive when we fail. People are quick to point out action that ends badly. But we rarely recognize the sin of omission. We criticize the guy who fed too much sugar to starving children rather than criticizing the thousands who fed them nothing.

The servant who buried his master's money rather than investing it like the other servants spared himself the embarrassment of a failed business venture. But his cowardice earned him the strongest rebuke: his master called him wicked, lazy, and worthless (Matt.

25:24–30). You don't want to be the servant who does nothing out of fear of messing up. You may well make a mistake through misguided action, but you're guaranteed to make a mistake by doing nothing.

Lisa and I have made mistakes by acting too quickly. Like the time we met a homeless woman with three kids and pregnant with her fourth. We quickly invited them to live with us. Her kids were out of control, bringing our own kids to tears. They wreaked havoc in our home and didn't seem to learn anything from their time with us. Then we discovered she was homeless only because she refused to follow her husband who loved her and wanted to be with her.

It might have been a mistake, but we don't regret trying. Our lives are full of successes and failures. To us, that's better than "playing it safe" by doing nothing. I'm sure we have made ten times as many mistakes by failing to act when we should have. So today, do *something*. We will all make mistakes. Err on the side of action.

Marriage Isn't that Great

MARRIAGE IN LIGHT OF GOD'S GLORY

Someone is watching you right now as you read this. Think about that. The God who loans you life sees your every move, hears each word you speak, and knows your every thought. And this is a good thing. You are seen by God. Noticed. *Known*.

God spoke, and the world came into existence. God spoke, and the world was demolished by a flood. One day, God will speak the only verdict that matters as He judges every person. This is the God who knows you, even now. This is the God who is watching you as you read.

I know this is supposed to be a book about marriage, but forget about people for a moment. Let's focus on something bigger: God. Focus on something more important: your relationship with God. This relationship is far more critical than your marriage, and it's everlasting.

This may come as a shock, but Jesus taught that marriages on earth don't carry over into heaven. In Matthew 22, Jesus was asked about a hypothetical widow who continues to remarry. The religious leaders of the day were asking Jesus which husband this woman would be married to in heaven. Jesus answered:

> "...in the resurrection they neither marry nor are
> given in marriage, but are like angels in heaven."
> (Matthew 22:30)

Maybe Jesus' statement is hard for you to accept. (Hopefully you're not rejoicing...) For me, it's hard to imagine the day when Lisa and I will no longer be married, but two thoughts bring me comfort. First, this doesn't mean that Lisa and I won't be deeply in love with each other in heaven. My guess is that I will be even closer to Lisa when we exist in glorified bodies absent of sin. Things must be different in order to be better. Second, I will have a union with God which is guaranteed to be better than any earthly closeness I might be experiencing now. I trust the God who created marriage when He promises a better future.

We all need to prioritize our eternal relationship with our Creator above all things. Besides, until you relate properly to God, you won't be much help to anyone else. People who aren't living well make matters worse by living together.

When two people are right with Him, they will be right with each other. As a pastor for over 20 years, I have come to the conclusion that most marriage problems are not really marriage problems. They are God problems. They can be traced back to one or both people having a poor relationship with God or a faulty understanding of Him. An accurate picture of God is vital to a healthy marriage. It's vital to everything. As A.W. Tozer put it, "All the problems of heaven and earth, though they were to confront us together and at once, would be nothing compared with that overwhelming problem of God: That He is; what He is like; and what we as moral beings must do about Him."[1]

Now that it's clear this chapter is about God, not marriage, you may be tempted to skip ahead to the "good stuff." After all, you and God are fine; you're just trying to work on your marriage. But don't be foolish. Don't assume that you are right with God. We cannot afford to be complacent about this relationship.

Almost everyone I meet believes they are headed for heaven. At every funeral I attend, a eulogy declares that the deceased is now "in a better place." But if this is true, why does Jesus talk about a narrow gate and a hard path?

> "Enter by the narrow gate. For the gate is wide and the way is easy that leads to destruction, and those who enter by it are many. For the gate is narrow and the way is hard that leads to life, and those who find it are few." (Matthew 7:13-14)

Jesus is clear: not everyone is headed for eternal life. Few find it.

So rather than jumping to the symptoms of an unhealthy marriage, let's focus on something more vital. This must be at the heart of our marriages because it makes a marriage either wonderful or destructive. Let's begin where the Bible tells us to begin:

The fear of the LORD is the beginning of wisdom.
(Psalm 111:10)

The fear of the LORD is the beginning of knowledge. (Proverbs 1:7)

The fear of the LORD leads to life. (Proverbs 19:23)

FEAR GOD

I'm guessing those are two words you didn't expect to read
in a marriage book. But nothing could be more foundational for
marriage. Without a healthy fear of God, we will not fully enjoy
life and love. Without it, our priorities will be completely off.
Yet if a healthy fear of God is at the foundation of who we are, a
beautiful life and marriage can be built upon this.

The LORD takes pleasure in those who fear Him.
(Psalm 147:11)

"And do not fear those who kill the body but cannot kill the soul. Rather fear him who can destroy
both soul and body in hell." (Matthew 10:28)

Most people underestimate how terrifying it will be to see
God. Hands down, it will be the most shocking moment of your
existence. And we can't ignore the fact that we could see Him

at any moment. What do you think you will feel when you see Him? I can pretty much guarantee you won't be thinking about your family.

While there's no way to know exactly how we will feel, Scripture contains stories of how other people responded when they caught a glimpse of Him. There was John, who collapsed like a corpse (Rev. 1:17). There was Isaiah, who cursed himself and declared his own sinfulness (Is. 6:5). There was Job, who immediately saw his own foolishness and said:

> "I had heard of you by the hearing of the ear,
>> but now my eye sees you;
> therefore I despise myself,
>> and repent in dust and ashes." (Job 42:5-6)

Each response differs, yet all are characterized by fear and awe. It would be foolish to think it will be any different for us.

And this is not just an Old Testament mindset. Compare Isaiah 2:17-19 with Revelation 6:15-16, and you will see that God did not become less terrifying in the New Testament.

> And the haughtiness of man shall be humbled,
>> and the lofty pride of men shall be brought low,
>> and the LORD alone will be exalted in that day.
> And the idols shall utterly pass away.
> And people shall enter the caves of the rocks
>> and the holes of the ground,

from before the terror of the LORD,
>   and from the splendor of his majesty,
>   when he rises to terrify the earth. (Isaiah 2:17-19)

Then the kings of the earth and the great ones
and the generals and the rich and the powerful,
and everyone, slave and free, hid themselves in
the caves and among the rocks of the mountains,
calling to the mountains and rocks, "Fall on us
and hide us from the face of him who is seated on
the throne, and from the wrath of the Lamb, for
the great day of their wrath has come, and who
can stand?" (Revelation 6:15-17)

Oddly, I meet very few people who think about that moment. Is it because we don't really believe it's going to happen? We think about upcoming vacations and imagine how much fun we will have. We think about upcoming trials and worry about how difficult they will be. Why don't we think about seeing God for the first time?

I try to think about it often because it keeps me centered. This is also why I imagine Lisa seeing God for the first time. I love her, so I want her to be ready for it.

Most of us get nervous in front of certain people, so how in the world can we prepare to meet the One who "dwells in unapproachable light" (1 Tim. 6:16)? Fortunately, the Bible was written for that very purpose.

STARE AT GOD

I was intimidated to introduce myself to Lisa for the first time. Twenty years later, that has changed significantly. I now feel more comfortable with her than with any other person on earth. Time in a person's presence changes everything. Relationship changes everything.

In Revelation 4, the Bible speaks of high angels who are in the presence of God. It says that "day and night they never cease to say, 'Holy, holy, holy is the Lord God Almighty, who was and is and is to come!" *All they ever do* is look at God and declare how holy He is. They're doing it right now. They'll be doing it when you put this book down, when you go to bed tonight, and when you wake up tomorrow. It's worth every moment of their time to be in His presence and proclaiming His greatness. So wouldn't it make sense to spend at least a small portion of your day doing the same? Have you done this yet today? God wants us to worship Him and thank Him all throughout our day (Eph. 5:18-20). If we don't stare at God, we'll spend our time staring at lesser things. Namely, ourselves.

This is the mistake a lot of couples make. They spend a lot of time looking at themselves and each other but very little time staring at God. When this is the focus, they naturally begin to structure every aspect of their lives around the few years they have with each other on earth, rather than the millions they will spend in His presence. Or away from His presence. These people live as though they are not dying. They live as though the King is not returning.

David had only one request:

> One thing have I asked of the LORD,
>> that will I seek after:
> that I may dwell in the house of the LORD
>> all the days of my life,
> to gaze upon the beauty of the LORD
>> and to inquire in his temple.
>
> (Psalm 27:4)

That's it. That's all he asked God for. He knew this was the answer to any problem he had.

Imagine standing beside the throne of God for a moment. One instant in His presence and everything feels small, insignificant. The silliness of the issues that grabbed our attentions and affections is exposed. So David tells God that all he wants is to see Him daily. To stare at Him.

If I could read a manuscript of your prayers over the past month, what would I see as the "one thing" you repeatedly ask for? Actually answer that. Our prayers reveal a lot about us. Our requests show us what we treasure, and our tone reveals our opinion of Him.

> God is in heaven and you are on earth. Therefore
> let your words be few. (Ecclesiastes 5:2)

You don't need to go looking for God. He's with you right now. Take time now to *be* with Him. To gaze at Him. To praise Him. This may be a completely new experience for you. Get alone with Him, asking for nothing. Read the description of God in Revelation 4 and 5 and picture Him as you enter His presence in prayer. Don't talk too much or ask for much. Just think about Him and tell Him how much you revere Him. Close your eyes and do it now.

If you just did that, I assume that you see the importance of focusing on God above all else. If every married person would do that regularly, many problems would disappear. Again, our marriage problems are not really marriage problems. They are heart problems. They are God problems. Our lack of intimacy with God causes a void that we try to fill with the frailest of substitutes. Like wealth or pleasure. Like fame or respect. Like people. Like marriage.

Few would deny that marriages are destroyed by selfishness. At times, we all over-value our own pursuits while ignoring the desires of God and others. But we can't cure our narcissism by trying to ignore ourselves. The solution is to stare at God. When we actually stare at Him, everything else fades to its proper place.

Not only does meditating on God create closeness with Him, but it rekindles our fear of Him. Sometimes, it's a healthy fear that protects our marriage when the feelings of closeness aren't there.

PROTECT YOUR MARRIAGE

Things are different nowadays. Sin is more accessible and acceptable. Two specific areas come to mind, both deadly to marriage: pornography and flirting.

When I was a kid, a guy had to let everyone in the store know he was a pervert when he walked to the counter to buy a Playboy magazine. These days, people can look endlessly at pornography on the privacy of their own phones. And many don't even consider that perverted. It's the norm!

When I was a kid, a woman would have to flirt with a man face to face, in a normal social setting. Once again, there was the shame of people seeing it and labeling her a "whore" or "slut." Now with Facebook and text messaging, women and men can approach each other in secret to test the waters. And the affairs that spring from it, as well as the divorces that result from it, have become more acceptable. Even in the church.

But some things never change. God still sees it. God still hates it as much as He ever has. Though the majority may support you now, God still does not. Excuses like "my husband doesn't pay attention to me" or "my wife has not been meeting my needs" are still not heard by God. Satan is still the source of those voices that tell you it's okay—even when those voices belong to your friends, counselors, or pastors.

And the answer to sin is still the same: Fear God. Love for your family is not always enough to protect your family from your own wickedness. It's a deep-rooted knowledge that a holy God is watching that will steer you from evil during the most alluring temptations.

> Do not be deceived: God is not mocked, for whatever one sows, that will he also reap. For the one who sows to his own flesh will from the flesh reap corruption, but the one who sows to the Spirit will from the Spirit reap eternal life. (Galatians 6:7-8)

> Therefore, my beloved, as you have always obeyed,
> so now, not only as in my presence but much more
> in my absence, work out your own salvation with
> fear and trembling. (Philippians 2:12)

Remember that there is an enemy who is seeking to destroy your marriage. Our battle is not against flesh and blood (Eph. 6:12), so we can't safeguard our marriages through more date nights, more vacations, or more counseling. Those things are not bad, but we have to see that there is more going on. Sincere and concentrated prayer will do infinitely more than any human strategy for a happy marriage. "The prayer of a righteous person has great power as it is working" (James 5:16).

The other source of power we must not neglect is the Bible. That phrase may sound like a broken record for those who grew up attending church services, but I hope you don't tune it out. The verses in the Bible are more than good teachings, they possess power. They are not just powerful points—they are living words, spoken by the same God whose words formed our universe.

> For the word of God is living and active, sharper
> than any two-edged sword, piercing to the divi-
> sion of soul and of spirit, of joints and of marrow,
> and discerning the thoughts and intentions of the
> heart. (Hebrews 4:12)

The words in your Bible carry an unparalleled power to penetrate to your very core. They reach beyond your self-deception, your hypocrisy, and your false motives and expose your soul. You sit down to read this book, and it tears you open, doing God's work in your heart and mind. We hear strong opinions from arrogant people all day long. We need to cleanse our minds by reminding each other of God's actual words.

Read these passages slowly and reverently. Read them aloud to yourself or to each other:

> Guard your steps when you go to the house of God. To draw near to listen is better than to offer the sacrifice of fools, for they do not know that they are doing evil. Be not rash with your mouth, nor let your heart be hasty to utter a word before God, for God is in heaven and you are on earth. Therefore let your words be few. For a dream comes with much business, and a fool's voice with many words. When you vow a vow to God, do not delay paying it, for he has no pleasure in fools. Pay what you vow. It is better that you should not vow than that you should vow and not pay. Let not your mouth lead you into sin, and do not say before the messenger that it was a mistake. Why should God be angry at your voice and destroy the work of your hands? For when dreams increase and words grow many, there is vanity; but God is the one you must fear. (Ecclesiastes 5:1–7)

> But the day of the Lord will come like a thief,
> and then the heavens will pass away with a roar,
> and the heavenly bodies will be burned up and
> dissolved, and the earth and the works that are
> done on it will be exposed. Since all these things
> are thus to be dissolved, what sort of people ought
> you to be in lives of holiness and godliness, wait-
> ing for and hastening the coming of the day of
> God, because of which the heavens will be set on
> fire and dissolved, and the heavenly bodies will
> melt as they burn! (2 Peter 3:10–12)

Verses like these need little explaining. The more we read them, the stronger our lives will be. The more we speak them to one another, the stronger our marriages will be. Protect your marriage by reminding each other that God is holy and Jesus *will* return at any moment.

We all have a tendency to look within ourselves for truth. In our arrogance, we like to believe that we can solve issues by thinking deeply. But the Bible insists that our best thoughts don't hold a candle to God's. So when it comes to marriage, or any issue at all, we should never rely on our wisdom. We cannot do better than listening to His words.

> For my thoughts are not your thoughts,
>   neither are your ways my ways, declares the LORD.

> For as the heavens are higher than the earth,
>> so are my ways higher than your ways
>> and my thoughts than your thoughts. (Isaiah 55:8–9)

If those verses are true, we should stop wasting time searching our own minds and spend our days studying His.

WORSHIP GOD, NOT MARRIAGE

When my computer sits idle for a few minutes, the screen saver displays a picture of our family running along the beach. As I look at it, it often leads me to worship. How did God come up with this? The imagination and power required to create people and design marriage is literally unfathomable. The creation of family was brilliant. To go through life not as individuals, but as groups that show each other love and support, that carry each other through the hard times and laugh together in the good times, that pray and praise and cry and suffer and enjoy *together*—who else could have come up with something that beautiful?

We have to be careful, though. While it is good to enjoy what God has created, the love of family can quickly eclipse all others.

When Jesus was asked what the most important command was, He said, "you shall love the Lord your God with all your heart and with all your soul and with all your mind. This is the great and first commandment" (Matt. 22:37–38). Jesus goes so far as to say, "Whoever loves son or daughter more than me is not worthy of me" (Matt. 10:37). Jesus is clear that He wants first place in our lives.

In fact, He also says, "If anyone comes to me and does not hate his own father and mother and wife and children and brothers and sisters, yes, and even his own life, he cannot be my disciple" (Luke 14:26). It's not that we should love Him a little more than we love our families; our love for Him should be in a different category. He is far beyond us, so our love for Him should be far beyond our love for others. The gap between our love for God and our love for our spouses should be massive. The two are not worthy of being compared. We normally order our affections like the list on the left, when the list on the right is the biblical mandate.

1. GOD	1. GOD
2. Family	
3. Friends	
4. Work	
5. Possessions	2. Family, Friends, Work, Possessions

Too many are content with the list as it is arranged on the left. But that list doesn't come from the Bible. In fact, it stands in opposition to what the Bible actually teaches. God demands that we treat Him as holy, which means "set apart." If we loved God the way we ought, there would be no such thing as a "close second."

Again, a lot of this will fall into place as you stare at Him. Consider your heart now. What is your first love? What do you pray for? What do you meditate on?

We were created by Him and for His glory.

> For by him all things were created, in heaven and on earth, visible and invisible, whether thrones or dominions or rulers or authorities—all things were created through him and for him. (Colossians 1:16)

> So, whether you eat or drink, or whatever you do, do all to the glory of God. (1 Corinthians 10:31)

THERE'S TOO MUCH AT STAKE —*Lisa*

In Philippians 3, Paul talks about the righteousness that comes through faith in Christ. He says, "Not that I have already obtained this or am already perfect, but I press on to make it my own, because Christ Jesus has made me his own" (v. 12). Here's the thing: *many* people forget that after the moment of salvation comes a lifetime of sanctification (the process of becoming holy). Your righteous position is gained in an instant of true belief, but your righteousness—your Christ-likeness—grows in depth over a lifetime of pursuing the things of God. That's why Paul longs to lay hold of all that Christ offers.

We cannot stop pressing on toward this goal in *every* area of our lives. And Christ-likeness may be *especially* important in our marriages because marriage is such a powerful way to display the gospel and the glory of God. It is the first place people will look to see if we really believe what we say we believe. Someone can have a dynamic speaking gift, or generously give to anyone in need, or appear to know a lot of Scripture, but if they have a terrible marriage, it raises questions. How can he treat his wife that way?

Why is she so disrespectful to her husband? They obviously do not believe what they claim to believe. It should burden us deeply that many of our marriages paint the gospel in a bad light.

Can you imagine if the divorce rate among Christians was next to nothing? What an incredible way to cry out to the world that *we are different!* We have the mind of Christ, we have the power of the Holy Spirit, we choose to die to ourselves and love and forgive even when things get difficult. This would turn heads. This is what God wants for us as His people.

> Do all things without grumbling or disputing, that you may be blameless and innocent, children of God without blemish in the midst of a crooked and twisted generation, among whom you shine as lights in the world… (Philippians 2:14–15)

Does your marriage stand out in this generation? This relationship was designed to reflect God's glory. We either shine a light that makes sense as a child of God or we take part in the crookedness and depravity of the world around us. In a way, if we don't get it right in our marriage relationships, it won't really matter how well we do beyond that.

Marriage is a big deal when you think of it that way. God does so much work in our minds and hearts through this relationship. Marriage is one of the most humbling, sanctifying journeys you will ever be a part of. It forces us to wrestle with our selfishness and pride. But it also gives us a platform to display love and commitment.

A quote I heard recently: "We are God's plan to make it believable that He is good and loving and true." God has always chosen to reveal Himself through people. Just as He used the nation of Israel to show the world who the one true God was, He calls us to represent Him to the world around us. Our lives should make it believable that there is a God. The way we love our spouses should make the love of Christ believable and true. Wouldn't it be incredible to know that your marriage actually *drew* someone into a relationship with Christ?

People need to see God in you, as you love your spouse. The world desperately needs to see an accurate reflection of Christ and the church in our marriages, because this is about God's glory! We need a fundamental shift in our thinking about what is at stake in the way we live our lives and the way we live out our marriages.

I read an amazing quote from our dear friend Joni Eareckson Tada. What she says transcends her own personal struggle with quadriplegia and chronic pain, and applies to *every* circumstance in our lives—whether painful or joyful. She said,

> "I realized that the stakes were far greater, far more immense and cosmic than merely my satisfaction with a wheelchair and its unpleasant baggage. I shifted my focus onto God. His glory was at stake, and that made my satisfaction in Him (not satisfaction with 'the way things were') the *real* issue. It was no longer a matter of being content with His plan for my life; it was a matter

of finding Him utterly and supremely the source
of all contentment. This, much to my delight,
would give Him the greatest glory."

What an incredible perspective. Regardless of how satisfying
your marriage is or isn't, the *real issue* is how satisfied you are with
Him. Whether your marriage is full of joy or pain, God's glory is
at stake. Do you need to shift your focus onto Him? To me, this
whole concept sums up our reason for writing this book.

There are *many, many* Christians caught up in their own
personal satisfaction, giving no thought to the way in which their
lives show a deep satisfaction in God. Where is the willingness
to forego a feeling of happiness in our marriages for the sake of
God's glory? No, we are clawing for our rights, and forgetting
that there is something far more immense and cosmic going on.

"Let your light shine before others, so that they
may see your good works and give glory to your
Father who is in heaven." (Matthew 5:16)

It has always been about the glory of God. Our lives and our
marriages can cause people to praise God! Especially now in the
midst of such selfishness and darkness and pride.

At one time you were darkness, but now you are
light in the Lord. Walk as children of light...
(Ephesians 5:8)

CONCLUSION

While the Bible helps us understand what marriage is and how it works, it is not a book about marriage. It is a book about God. It teaches us about our Creator by revealing His character, describing His past actions, and telling us His future plans. When we consider the biblical storyline as a whole, our over-prioritization of our human relationships looks absurd. The Bible begins with a Being so powerful that His words command non-existent things to exist, and they obey. It presents to us a Being so holy and just that He once drowned every person on earth, sparing only the eight people who still looked to Him. This book is full of examples of God punishing the arrogant and blessing the humble. And the Bible concludes with visions of a terrifying future judgment, where every person is cast eternally into either a place of perfect pleasure in union with God or a place of ultimate pain apart from Him.

God takes center stage in every story of Scripture. He is the Creator of life, the Judge, and the Savior. So while the Bible does talk about marriage, let's be careful not to use the Bible just to find helpful tips on marriage. There is a much, much bigger picture.

Draw close to Him and let your marriage be the overflow of that. When things are right with God, your marriage can actually become what it was designed to be. Peace comes when both parties come to an agreement. Agree on God—agree on His holiness and the supremacy He deserves in your lives.

DO SOMETHING

The important thing is that you respond to the truth in this chapter. Below are some of our suggestions to help you do that. If these help you fear God and exalt Him to His proper place in your life and in your marriage, then act on them! If you have something better or more specific that will help you do this, then do that instead. The important thing is that you do *something*.

MAKE A TIMELINE OF YOUR RELATIONSHIP.

+ *Start by describing what you were each like when you first met.*

+ *Also describe what you are each like now. How have you grown or regressed over the course of your relationship?*

+ *Then look forward 10 years. If your marriage were to be exactly what you want it to be in 10 years, what would it look like?*

+ *Now, considering Point A (where your relationship started) and Point B (where you stand right now), what steps will you need to take to get to Point C (where you want to be in 10 years)? What sacrifices will you need to make? What habits and pursuits will you need to cultivate? Which will you need to do away with? How can you help each other along this path?*

ANALYZE YOUR FEAR OF THE LORD.

✦ *Describe how each of you fears the Lord, right now, at this moment. Describe the ways in which your fear of the Lord is strong and appropriate, and the ways in which you don't fear the Lord as you ought.*

✦ *Help each other with your descriptions. Be sure that your description is accurate by switching lists and giving each other comments.*

✦ *Strategize how you can help each other develop in your fear of the Lord. What passages of Scripture can you read together to reinforce this? How can you pray for one another? What evidence should you be looking for to indicate that each of you is indeed growing in the fear of the Lord?*

Pursue the Perfect Marriage

MARRIAGE IN LIGHT OF THE GOSPEL

I was recently at lunch with a friend who was telling me about his parents. His dad is 95 and his mom is 96. They fell in love in the sixth grade and have now been married for 75 years. They have been best friends for 83 years! He proceeded to tell me that his mom's mind is now slipping away, but his dad simply sits next to her for hours at a time with his hand resting gently on her arm. Picture that scene for a moment.

I wonder what goes through his mind when he sits beside her. What must he think and feel when he reaches out and makes contact with that arm that has been beside him for 83 years? What would it be like to share 83 years of memories with another person? I picture these stored up memories like a photo album and I imagine these two flipping through page after page, remembering scenes of laughing together on a playground, falling in love, getting married, having kids, having grandkids, and having great grandkids. The emotional depth must be intensified by scenes of arguments and tragedies, loss and heartbreak. I imagine them flipping the final pages leading up to the back cover, where scenes of these two finishing their life on earth side by side will one day be placed.

In an age of disposable marriages, it's nice to get a snapshot of commitment, longevity, and some of the beauty God intended for marriage. And it's nice to know that these models exist, even if we never meet them. It gives us something to aim for. It makes me anticipate the future with my wife. Occasionally, Lisa complains about getting old, and points out the wrinkles on her face. I now tell her how much I love them because they're a reminder that we are growing old together—our dream come true. I'd love to have 83 years of memories with her. I doubt it will happen, though—as that would put me at 108.

The story of this elderly couple appeals to us because we were designed for relationship. God said, "It is not good that the man should be alone" (Gen. 2:18). Anyone who has experienced the pain of loneliness feels that truth. So much of the pleasure we find in life comes in the context of healthy relationships. Marriage is absolutely brilliant. And yet, as beautiful as marriage can be, by design it is a mere shadow of something much greater.

THE MIRACULOUS MARRIAGE

In Ephesians 5, Paul says that marriage is a "mystery." But then he explains that the mystery is not marriage between a man and a woman, but the marriage between Christ and the church. It is a miracle that human beings can be united with God!

> "Therefore a man shall leave his father and mother and hold fast to his wife, and the two shall become one flesh." *This mystery* is profound, and I am saying that *it refers to Christ and the church.* (Ephesians 5:31–32, emphasis added)

God pursues human beings! This is seen throughout Scripture. We see God walking in the garden with Adam and Eve. We hear God speaking to Moses on a mountaintop. We find His mysterious presence in the tabernacle and the temple. When we come to the New Testament, we read about the birth of Jesus—*Immanuel*, a title that literally means "God with us"—and we see Him walking amongst His wayward people. Later, He sends His Holy Spirit to actually live inside of His people, both as individuals and collectively as His church. Finally, the Bible describes the future, when Jesus marries His people and lives with them forever.

The Bible reveals the most breath-taking possibility: the union of man with God.

> God shows his love for us in that while we were still sinners, Christ died for us... For if while we were enemies we were reconciled to God by the death of his Son, much more, now that we are reconciled, shall we be saved by his life. (Romans 5:8–10)

The staggering part is that God doesn't just permit us to know Him, He sacrificed deeply to make it happen! God doesn't simply leave an invitation on the table—He paid the highest possible price to make it a reality.

There is no greater love story. The Judge of the universe chased after those who rebelled against Him. People made themselves God's enemies by rejecting His rule and following their own desires. Yet God so loves His "enemies" that He sent His Son to pay the penalty for their crimes. God's wrath was satisfied as Jesus hung on the cross. Through His death, believers are cleared of their sin and reconciled to the God they once rejected. This makes God both fair and forgiving, just and justifier (see Rom. 3:21–26). He is just because His judgment against our sin was carried out. We are justified because His innocent Son suffered on our behalf.

As I write this, it feels cheap. I'm trying to describe something so sacred with lifeless words on a page. My words feel so subdued. So sterile. I want to stop writing, stare you in the face, and scream: Jesus died! He chose the most grueling death to bring you to God! Everything is changed! You and I were destined for a horrifying encounter with God—we were "objects of wrath" (Eph. 2:3)—but that has all changed! Death no longer scares me! I can't wait to die! Thank you Jesus!!!

YOU ARE SO BEAUTIFUL

It's not just that I'm no longer dirty as I stand before God. What He did on our behalf does not make us spiritually neutral.

Rather, He has made us righteous. Attractive. Those who cling to Jesus are beautiful to Him.

> I will greatly rejoice in the Lord;
> my soul shall exult in my God,
> for he has clothed me with the garments of salvation;
> he has covered me with the robe of righteousness,
> as a bridegroom decks himself like a priest with a beautiful headdress, and as a bride adorns herself with her jewels. (Isaiah 61:10)

He makes us beautiful, even comparing us to a bride on her wedding day! I've had the privilege of performing many weddings, and it's always a cool moment when the groom sees his bride for the first time. I usually hear the word "wow" as she enters the room in her wedding dress. He knew she was going to look beautiful, but there is genuine surprise in his voice and on his face as he sees her beauty on their wedding day.

Let this sink in: God uses *that* picture to describe how attractive we are to Him. He has made us *that* beautiful. It's hard to imagine the Creator of the universe looking at us with *that* kind of fondness. Some of us are overjoyed just to know that He doesn't hate us! So it's a real struggle to believe that we are stunningly attractive to Him.

Just remember that it's nothing we did. Jesus took away all of our ugliness. Unlike a typical bride, we are all shabby, grotesque, and woefully unprepared moments before we walk down the aisle.

But our Groom beautifies us when we look to Him in faith, and in that instant we become His cherished bride.

> For our sake he made him to be sin who knew no
> sin, so that in him we might become the righteous-
> ness of God. (2 Corinthians 5:21)

We are the bride of Christ now, but the Bible also describes us as waiting with anticipation for the "marriage of the Lamb." Think of how much time, money, and effort goes into our wedding ceremonies. But *this* is the marriage that Scripture emphasizes, so this should be the marriage that we are obsessed with. We are the bride—we have been reconciled with God and we currently enjoy a relationship with Him—but the actual wedding is still to come.

The New Testament often presents a tension between what is ("already") and what will be ("not yet"). Jesus is the King now, but His full reign awaits the future. Jesus dealt Satan a fatal blow, but He will not dispose of Satan entirely until His second coming. We are the bride of Christ now, but the full consummation awaits His return:

> Then I heard what seemed to be the voice of a great
> multitude, like the roar of many waters and like the
> sound of mighty peals of thunder, crying out,
> > "Hallelujah!
> > For the Lord our God
> > > the Almighty reigns.

> Let us rejoice and exult
>   and give him the glory,
> for the marriage of the Lamb has come,
>   and his Bride has made herself ready;
> it was granted her to clothe herself
>   with fine linen, bright and pure"—
> for the fine linen is the righteous deeds of the
>   saints.
> And the angel said to me, "Write this: Blessed
>   are those who are invited to the marriage
>   supper of the Lamb." And he said to
>   me, "These are the true words of God."
> (Revelation 19:6–9)

This is the destiny of all who believe in Jesus. The marriage ceremony is followed by God living with us in a way that none of us has ever experienced. In our eternal future, there will no longer be any death, pain, sickness, or crying (Rev. 21:1-4). Our time on earth is brief and trying. Our time in the new heavens and new earth will be eternal and glorious.

If this is the first time you've understood what God has done for you, stay focused on this one point. There's no sense in improving your marriage until you are secure with God. Find a quiet place and talk to your Creator. Confess your sins to Him, ask for forgiveness. Thank Him for dying for you. Tell Him that you want His Spirit to live within you. Turn from your old way of life and follow Him, living in light of eternity.

> If we confess our sins, he is faithful and just to for-
> give us our sins and to cleanse us from all unrigh-
> teousness. (1 John 1:9)

If you have been familiar with these truths for years, don't let this good news become old news. Even now, your union with God should fascinate you more than anything else on earth.

FAILURE IS IMPOSSIBLE

Picture a 100 meter race. I'm on the starting blocks and I'm racing my dad. One second into the race, it should be obvious that I am going to win. The main reason: my dad died years ago. I know, it's a creepy illustration, but hang with me.

My point is that being alive gives us a tremendous advantage. The Bible says *we were dead* in our sins, just like everyone else in the world (Eph. 2:1–3). The imagery is of a few living people walking around a bunch of corpses; like a theological zombie film. This is how we are to appear in comparison to the world! Too many Christians are content with appearing to be a bit more moral than the people around them. But the difference between a true Christian and a non-Christian is not about subtle moral distinctions—it's the difference between being alive and being dead!

Take a moment to set down this book and read Ezekiel 37:1–14. Trust me, you won't regret it. In this passage, the prophet Ezekiel stands in the middle of a valley. As he looks around, he sees that the valley is covered with human bones. They are everywhere, and they are dry and brittle. And then God commands Ezekiel to speak:

"Prophesy over these bones, and say to them, O dry bones, hear the word of the Lord. Thus says the Lord God to these bones: Behold, I will cause breath to enter you, and you shall live. And I will lay sinews upon you, and will cause flesh to come upon you, and cover you with skin, and put breath in you, and you shall live, and you shall know that I am the Lord." (Ezekiel 37:4–6)

As Ezekiel speaks these words to the dry bones around him, he hears a sound, then a rattling, and then he looks out to see the bones coming together, sinews attaching, and skin covering the once-decayed bodies. Then God breathes life into these bodies, and "they lived and stood on their feet, an exceedingly great army" (v. 10).

This is the difference between those who have been made alive in Christ, and those who have not. A resurrected being versus a pile of dry, brittle bones.

One chapter earlier, God had promised through Ezekiel that He would come to His people, transplant their stone hearts for living hearts, and put His very Spirit inside them (Ezek. 36:25–27).

This leads us to the first chapters of Acts, where the disciples of Jesus were mysteriously filled with the Spirit and received tremendous power. The onlookers that day saw the immediate transformation. Peter then told them that the same thing could happen to them!

Peter said to them, "Repent and be baptized every one of you in the name of Jesus Christ for the forgiveness of your sins, and you will receive the gift of the Holy Spirit. For the promise is for you and for your children and for all who are far off, everyone whom the Lord our God calls to himself." (Acts 2:38–39)

That day 3,000 people were baptized. But notice the phrase: *The promise is for you* and *for your children* and *for all who are far off.* What the disciples experienced that day—the beginnings of Ezekiel's vision of a once-dead but now alive and powerful army— was offered to those who witnessed the Spirit's power in Acts 2. And it would still be available to their children. And it awaits all those who are far off. God is still calling people to Himself. You and I can have the same power that the disciples experienced two thousand years ago through the Holy Spirit.

So the question is: Is He in you? Have you chosen to "repent and be baptized" and "receive the gift of the Holy Spirit"? Remember that this is the difference between life and death, between scattered bones and living being.

It could be possible that the Lord is using your marriage to call you to Himself. Maybe you were just looking for tips on marriage, but God had a much bigger plan in mind. If you believe in what Jesus has done for you and haven't done this yet, find a Bible teaching church where someone can baptize you and help you understand the teachings of Christ.

When Lisa and I began kicking around ideas for this book, we agreed that it would be pointless to cast a vision of a healthy marriage to those who don't possess the Holy Spirit. The Spirit doesn't merely increase your odds of success. Remember, this is the difference between being dead and being alive. Without the Spirit of God, it doesn't matter how healthy your view of marriage is or how badly you want it. A dead spouse cannot conjure up a living marriage.

Put simply: the Holy Spirit moves us from an impossible situation into a position where it is impossible to fail. Meditate on the following verses, which some consider to be the most important in Scripture:

> For those who live according to the flesh set their minds on the things of the flesh, but those who live according to the Spirit set their minds on the things of the Spirit. For to set the mind on the flesh is death, but to set the mind on the Spirit is life and peace. For the mind that is set on the flesh is hostile to God, for it does not submit to God's law; indeed, it cannot. Those who are in the flesh cannot please God.
>
> You, however, are not in the flesh but in the Spirit, if in fact the Spirit of God dwells in you. Anyone who does not have the Spirit of Christ does not belong to him. But if Christ is in you, although the body is dead because of sin, the Spirit is life because of righteousness. If the Spirit of him who raised Jesus from the dead dwells in you, he who raised Christ Jesus from the dead will also give life to your mortal bodies through his Spirit who dwells in you. (Romans 8:5–11)

This passage makes me think of a Gatorade commercial. The commercial asks, "Is it in you?" as it shows athletes performing incredible feats while Gatorade comes sweating out of their pores. I love the visual illustration of something fueling us so powerfully from the inside that its presence is tangible and indisputable. Of course, Gatorade isn't really that powerful, and I don't need Gatorade to dominate on the basketball court. But the visual reminds me of the biblical description of the Holy Spirit.

God promises that an internal change—a new act of creation (2 Cor. 5:17)—will take place within those who believe. And that inward change will produce external actions. The Spirit fuels us so powerfully from the inside that His active presence is tangible and indisputable (see Gal. 5:22–24). If the actions aren't pouring out of your life, you have to ask yourself: Is He in you?

It's the good tree that can't help but bear good fruit (Matt. 7:16–20). It's out of the overflow of the heart that the mouth speaks (Luke 6:45). It's the presence of the Holy Spirit in the core of our beings that causes us to hate evil and love what is right (Rom. 8:9-17).

Once this internal change takes place, it's as if you can't keep yourself from acting. That is how the Christian life is supposed to work. Something wells up inside and gushes out. I don't conjure up love for Him; I love Him. I don't convince myself to serve Him; I'm compelled to serve Him. It's like I can't help but love people and sacrifice for the poor. There's a desire within me to do these things, and the actions flow from every fiber of my being. I hate lust. I hate pride. I hate *hate*, and I don't even try to. It's just who

I am. I no longer see His rules as burdens, I'm grateful to God for them. I have become a slave of righteousness, and I love it!

> But thanks be to God, that you who were once slaves of sin have become obedient *from the heart* to the standard of teaching to which you were committed, and, having been set free from sin, have become slaves of righteousness. (Romans 6:17–18, emphasis added)

Some believers today wish they could have lived in Old Testament times so they could experience God's power in the temple. Other believers wish they lived during Jesus' earthly ministry so they could speak to Jesus and see His miracles. Yet Jesus said that what we have now is better than either of those options.

> "I tell you the truth: *it is to your advantage that I go away*, for if I do not go away, the Helper will not come to you. But if I go, I will send him to you." (John 16:7, emphasis added)

If you find yourself wishing you could walk with Jesus or experience God's power in the temple, then something is wrong with your understanding and experience of the Holy Spirit.

We live during an amazing time in human history. This period where the Spirit of God dwells within believers is not a cheap substitute for the temple or Jesus. If anything, Scripture teaches that we have it better than the believers before us. God is not just with us, He is in us! This is why people shake their heads in disbelief when they hear Christians claim such power yet display such weak and unloving marriages.

If the Spirit of God is really inside of us, then His power will be *obvious* in our marriages. I'm tired of reading new statistics that show no difference between Christian marriages and non-Christian marriages. The solution doesn't come through trying harder or implementing the right strategies. It comes through the Spirit's power gushing out of our hearts, into our marriages, and into every aspect of our lives.

OUR ROLE IN HIS STORY

Have you ever considered the fact that you get to play a role in God's story? Take it one step further: Have you ever marveled at this? God created the world, and the people rebelled against God. So God sent prophets to warn His people, priests to intercede for His people, and kings to lead His people, but few turned back to God. So eventually God sent His Son to direct His people, but very few listened even to Him. Then Jesus died to pay for the sins of humanity, rose from the grave, and ascended to heaven where He reigns with the Father. When He left earth, Jesus sent the Holy Spirit to dwell within believers to empower them to continue Jesus' mission on earth.

So before the end of human history when the Savior and Judge will return to save and to judge, you were born. You are now called by God to showcase the power of His Spirit by the way you live. Your mission is to do this until He calls you home or returns to end human history, and you will then be rewarded—by the God who created you, the Son who died for you, and the Spirit who empowered you—for giving the world an accurate picture of His love. All of this culminates in the marriage of the Lamb, where you will join every believer throughout all time as the bride and be married to the only true King, with whom you will live and reign throughout all eternity.

That is the story into which we have been called. Each of us plays a tiny but significant role. Our marriages also play a significant role in His great plan. We are called to paint such an attractive picture of marriage that it causes people to long for the coming marriage with Jesus. God calls us to display the love and humility of Christ through our marriages. We will explore what this looks like later. For now, consider this: your current marriage plays a part in God's eternal plan.

Part of our role as Christians is to tell people about God's story. All of us should be regularly telling people about who Jesus is and what He has done. This is necessary, and we must never be ashamed of Jesus (Matt. 10:32–33). But it's one thing to *preach the gospel* and another thing to *display the gospel*.

In fact, displaying the gospel is the point of the church—the church exists to put God's attributes on display. We can talk about the forgiveness of Christ, but in the church we *demonstrate* the forgiveness of Christ. Jesus washed the disciples' feet, then He turned and told them to do the same (John 13:14–15). We are to imitate the actions of Jesus so that the world can see Him.

Consider this: the phrase "one another" is mentioned 59 times in the New Testament. Fifty-nine times, the writers of the New

Testament give us commands that we cannot obey without turning to another member of the church and demonstrating the character of God. It's impossible to "one another" yourself; it's impossible to "one another" in your heart. These "one another" commands require us to *demonstrate* the gospel with others.

While Jesus was on earth, He revealed God to the world. But now He has formed the church, given us His mission, and empowered us through the Holy Spirit. It's our job to reveal God to the world through the way we live together. In fact, Jesus said that the unity of His followers would confirm to the world that He was sent by God. I'm not exaggerating, look it up: John 17:20–23.

Displaying God to the world is the purpose of the church, and it's also the purpose of marriage. People should see the way I serve my wife and get a glimpse of the humility that Christ showed. Anyone who sees Lisa joyfully following my lead should understand more deeply what it means for the church to follow Christ out of their respect and trust for Him. God created marriage to be a picture that displays Christ to the world.

My point in all of this is to insist that there's more at stake in your marriage than just your marriage. The beauty of the gospel is at stake.

MARRIAGE & WEAKNESS —Lisa

I am so quick to say that I want to be Christ-like. My mind immediately thinks of His love, kindness, healings, and teachings—all things I long to exemplify. But I am struck by everything else it means to be Christ-like: humility, sacrifice, forgiveness, and suffering. These are things that are hard to exemplify, things that we often avoid.

This is why Jesus told people to count the cost of following Him. When great crowds would gather to see and hear Him, He knew that many were there for the show. They didn't want to hear Jesus say, "deny yourself, take up your *cross* and follow me." Many were not ready for Jesus to tell them that unless they were willing to give up *everything they had*, they were not worthy to be His disciples (Luke 14:33). Jesus wanted everyone to re-think their enthusiasm for Him.

> "A servant is not greater than his master." (John 13:16)

Why do we, as servants of Christ, assume that our lives will be free of sacrifice and suffering? If Jesus laid down His life, we must be ready to do the same. He left an example for us to *follow*. John says, "whoever says he abides in him ought to walk in the same way in which he walked" (1 John 2:6). Claiming to be a Christian means nothing if I don't embrace *everything* it means to be Christ-like.

Picture yourself sitting in that crowd that Jesus is speaking to. You may have gone to hear Him out of desperation, or even just hype. But as you listen to Him, your spirit is leaping. Suddenly you hear Him say, "Whoever does not bear his own cross and come after me cannot be my disciple" (Luke 14:27). Will you do it?

In the middle of an amazing marriage will you put your eyes on the Giver, rather than the gift? In the midst of a difficult marriage will you suffer for the sake of righteousness? Are you willing to follow the example of Christ, to walk in a manner *worthy* of the calling to which you have been called (Eph. 4:1)? You have been called to be Christ-like, and praise God He does not call us to something He is not fully able to realize in us. You may not *feel* like being Christ-like, but you have been *called* to it.

I don't know why we think we should always feel good or strong or able or ready. Very often, we know the path we ought to take—whether in marriage or some other area of life—yet we fail to act because we're not "feeling it."

If there's one thing I positively know, it's that feelings cannot be trusted. Not for a second. Too often, feelings are based on perceptions, self-preservation, fears, and emotion.

I once saw a bumper sticker that said, "Don't believe every-thing you think." I know—it's a bumper sticker. But it's still profound. You may *think* that you are weak. You may *think* there is no hope. You may *think* that you should always feel like obeying God, but you shouldn't believe everything you think.

> [God] said to me, "My grace is sufficient for you, for my power is made perfect in weakness." Therefore I will boast all the more gladly of my weaknesses, so that the power of Christ may rest upon me. For the sake of Christ, then, I am content with weaknesses, insults, hardships, persecutions, and calamities. For when I am weak, then I am strong. (2 Corinthians 12:9–10)

I find it so incredible that our sense of weakness and desperation is *exactly* when God's grace becomes most sufficient. To think that God's strength is so great that Paul would actually boast in his weakness rather than crumbling in it—this type of thinking should change us deeply.

Many times we recognize our weakness, but we fail to recognize what God can accomplish through it. It's a giving up point for far too many people who claim to know the all-powerful God. "I just can't" is a foolish statement for those who know God; it should not be in our vocabulary. "I can't" should be replaced by "I can do all things through him who strengthens me" (Phil. 4:13). Weakness should cause us to surrender to Christ in a way we never have before, to cry out to the One who has also known weakness, who has been tempted in every way, who knows the pull to give up, to move on, to pursue His own way.

> For we do not have a high priest who is unable to sympathize with our weaknesses, but one who in every respect has been tempted as we are, yet without sin. (Hebrews 4:15)

When you are weak, He is strong. When you feel like giving up, He shows you how to be faithful.

At the heart of the gospel is victory. Victory over judgment. Victory over death. Victory over sin.

Listen carefully here, because I'm afraid we'll lose those of you who have seen so much defeat, you have unknowingly stopped believing that victory is possible. Every person has the choice to think and act and respond in light of the gospel. It's true that a marriage can fail because of one person's refusal to do this. But it's also quite possible for a marriage to thrive because of only one person's commitment to do this. Ultimate victory is knowing that *you* have honored Christ at any cost, and your conscience is at rest in His presence.

> Consider him who endured from sinners such hostility against himself, so that you may not grow weary or fainthearted. In your struggle against sin you have not yet resisted to the point of shedding your blood. (Hebrews 12:3–4)

Some of the most beautiful, Spirit-filled people I know have experienced deep heartache in their marriages. The connection is not lost on me. I have witnessed how these same people have experienced such intimacy with their Savior as they wrestled through pain, forgiveness, and humility. Paul urges us, "let us not grow weary of doing good, for in due season we will reap, if we do not give up" (Gal. 6:9). I have actually seen these amazing people reap the harvest of radiating the love of Christ. The peace and joy that pours out of their lives is a living testimony that indeed, God's grace has been sufficient for them.

My heart longs to see God's people living in the power and victory of the gospel. We have to stop underestimating our God! Peter reminds us that "His divine power has granted to us *all things that pertain to life and godliness*" (2 Pet. 1:3, emphasis added). Yes, apart from Christ, we are weak and sinful. But connected to Christ we have everything we need to live a godly life. Peter tells everyone:

> "make every effort to supplement your faith with virtue, and virtue with knowledge, and knowledge with self-control, and self-control with steadfastness, and steadfastness with godliness, and godliness with brotherly affection, and brotherly affection with love. For if these qualities are yours and are increasing, they keep you from being ineffective or unfruitful in the knowledge of our Lord Jesus Christ." (2 Pet. 1:5–8)

It is possible to be ineffective and unfruitful in our knowledge of Jesus. I don't want that. I hope you don't either.

I keep thinking that the only way to "increase" in these qualities, or to "increase" in our Christ-likeness, is to increase our time and effort in pursuit of Him. To drastically increase the amount of time we spend in prayer. This is hard. I recognize how many things demand our constant attention. Sometimes I feel like I am just a moment away from operating out of the flesh. I can ride the wave of a good quiet time with Jesus for a day or two, maybe even a week! But then that inner struggle picks up. The further out of step I get with the Holy Spirit, the weaker I become spiritually. If I am going to become Christ-like, I really have to stay close to Christ. I also have to remember that Jesus said,

"This is my commandment, that you love one another
as I have loved you. Greater love has no one than this,
that someone lay down his life for his friends. You are
my friends if you do what I command you." (John
15:12–14)

The kind of love that brought Christ to the cross was not
easy for Him or painless. In fact, He wrestled and agonized with
His Father to see if there was any other way. Great love came at
a great price. We want our marriages to be filled with love, but
maybe we've forgotten the best way to accomplish that: display
the gospel. Lay down your very life for your husband or wife, but
ultimately, for Christ. Are you willing to die? Jesus is saying to
us, right now, in this moment of time: "If anyone would come
after me, let him deny himself, and take up his cross daily, and
follow me." (Luke 9:23)

CONCLUSION

Life is about Jesus. We are not here to tell our story, but His. We
are here to live His story, not ours.

What is your life? For you are a mist that appears for
a little time and then vanishes. (James 4:14)

So how will you spend your vapor of a life? And how will you
spend that one portion of your vapor that we call marriage? Will
you try to make your life call attention to itself? Or will you put
every ounce of effort into calling attention to the God who alone is

worthy of glory? You have a part to play in His story. Your marriage has a part to play. But all of it—your life, your marriage—will be lost in utter insignificance unless you spend it for His glory.

I have been loved, pursued, and saved by Almighty God. He gave up His life on the cross to bring me to God, and He now fills me with His Holy Spirit. I will one day be swept away by Jesus into a glorious eternity. But for now I am on a mission to tell His story to others. All of these truths make my life radically different from the person who doesn't believe these things.

Christ came so that we would "have life and have it abundantly" (John 10:19). When we are filled with His abundant life, we overflow. We have plenty to give others. That is how marriage is supposed to work: we find our identity and fulfillment in Christ, we fill to overflowing with the fruit of the Spirit, and then we pour that love, joy, peace, patience, kindness, and gentleness onto our spouses. He fills us up so much that we don't complain that others aren't meeting our needs. He gives us more good than we can handle. We spend our lives blessing others with the blessings we receive.

The Lord is my shepherd; I shall not want. (Psalm 23:1)

DO SOMETHING

We've just covered a lot of ground. Though we still haven't gotten very practical with regards to how your marriage should function, we've given you a lot to think about in terms of how the gospel should transform your marriage. Now it's time to respond.

SPEND SOME TIME WITH GOD.

✦ *Find a place where you won't be interrupted, and simply sit in His presence.*

✦ *Speak honestly to God about your fears for your marriage, the guilt from your past, your distrust of Him—anything. Lay it out there.*

✦ *Then spend some time thanking Him for the power of His gospel, for His strength in your weakness. Thank Him for His free gift of transforming grace.*

MAKE A GOSPEL LIST.

✦ *Make a list of what Jesus has done for you. What did He do? What are the implications of this? How is your life changed through what He has done? This shouldn't be a short list!*

✦ *Then make a list of ways the gospel should transform your marriage. How should Jesus' sacrificial example affect the way you relate to your spouse? How should the gift of the Holy Spirit revitalize your marriage? Include both big picture realities (like "this gives me strength when I don't feel like serving") and specific action steps (like "this will enable me to speak kindly to my spouse when _____").*

Learn to Fight Well

MARRIAGE IN LIGHT OF CHRIST'S EXAMPLE

We live in a time when Christians need to be told that they are supposed to live like Christ. That's weird. What's crazier is that people actually fight against this notion. "Christians" have come up with clever ways to explain why the followers of a suffering servant should live like kings. I honestly don't expect you to simply accept my (apparently unbelievable) assertion that *Christians* should look like *Christ*. I encourage you to read the New Testament and come to your own conclusions.

It's comforting to know that this is not a new struggle. John saw the need to remind believers that "whoever says he abides in him ought to walk in the same way in which he walked" (1 John 2:6). Paul encountered this problem when he chose to suffer like Christ while other self-appointed "apostles" chose to receive honor and riches. He had to call the believers in Corinth to "be imitators of me, as I am of Christ" (1 Cor. 11:1). Note Paul's sarcasm as he shows them how different he and the other apostles, who were following Jesus' example, looked compared to these believers who were choosing to follow the false teachers into luxury:

> Already you have all you want! Already you have become rich! Without us you have become kings! And would that you did reign, so that we might share the rule with you! For I think that God has exhibited us apostles as last of all, like men sentenced to death, because we have become a spectacle to the world, to angels, and to men. We are fools for Christ's sake, but you are wise in Christ. We are weak, but you are strong. You are held in honor, but we in disrepute. To the present hour we hunger and thirst, we are poorly dressed and buffeted and homeless, and we labor, working with our own hands. When reviled, we bless; when persecuted, we endure; when slandered, we entreat. We have become, and are still, like the scum of the world, the refuse of all things… I urge you, then, be imitators of me. (1 Corinthians 4:8–13, 16)

Jesus was clear that following Him meant—get this—following Him. The church has put so much effort into inventing a new form of "following Christ" that doesn't require imitating Him. We teach that even though Jesus allowed His rights to be trampled, we should fight for ours. We teach that even though Jesus lived simply, we have the right to live luxuriously (some prefer the term "comfortably"). Even as we teach that Jesus was rejected by the world, we pursue popularity. Ever wonder how many followers Jesus would have on Twitter? Or how many "likes" his Facebook posts would receive?

> "If the world hates you, know that it has hated me before it hated you... Remember the word that I said to you: 'A servant is not greater than his master.' If they persecuted me, they will also persecute you." (John 15:18, 20)

Look up these statements by Jesus if you are not convinced: Matthew 7:13-23, 8:18-22, 10:16-39, 19:23-30, 25:31-46; Mark 8:34-38, 10:24-45, 13:9-13; Luke 6:20-49, 9:21-27, 12:49-53, 13:22-30, 14:26-35, 17:22-37, 18:18-30, 21:10-19; John 6:52-69, 15:18-25, 16:1-4, 16:33.

Jesus spoke not only about His own suffering, but also the suffering His followers would face. As we read the book of Acts, we find the early Christians suffering, just as Jesus said they would. They don't seem to find this persecution surprising; rather, they see their suffering in light of Jesus' suffering (1 Peter 3:13–18). In fact, Peter lets us know what we should be expecting:

> Beloved, do not be surprised at the fiery trial when it comes upon you to test you, as though something strange were happening to you. But rejoice insofar as you share Christ's sufferings... (1 Peter 4:12–13)

From Acts through Revelation, you will find the apostles repeating these same teachings of Christ. The point is clear throughout the New Testament: followers of Christ are to imitate Christ. And because God has given us the invaluable gift of the Holy Spirit, we are given the ability and desire to become like Christ. The question, then, is whether or not we really want to become like Him.

DO YOU WANT TO BE AS HUMBLE AS JESUS?

We don't have time in this book to go through all of the attributes of Jesus, so we wanted to focus on one. Both Lisa and I believe that more than any other attribute of Jesus, His humility is the key to a healthy marriage. If two people make it their goal to imitate the humility of Christ, everything else will take care of itself. It really is that simple. Arguments escalate when we want to be right more than we want to be Christ. It is easy to get blinded in the heat of disagreements. Soon, all we want is to win, even if victory requires sin. The one who wins the argument is usually the one who acts less like Christ.

Every marriage goes through moments of anger and temporary failures. But you must determine your goal. What matters most: winning arguments or resembling Christ? Even in the heat of an argument we should be asking ourselves if we are acting like Jesus.

I'll admit it: I love winning. When I lose in sports, I lose sleep also. I stay up thinking about what I could have done differently. I hate losing. When I lose an argument, I think of things I should have said. It's a great feeling to say something that silences your opponent.

One of the first arguments Lisa and I had was about miniature golf. We were talking on the phone and trying to figure out what to do on Friday night. We were going out with two other couples and she suggested that we play miniature golf. I told her that wouldn't be the best because they will not let six people play together. We would have to split into two groups. To which she answered, "Well, that's stupid. Are you sure? That doesn't make any sense."

A wise man would have just left it alone, but I went on to explain why it did make sense that a group of six would move more slowly than two groups of three. She made it clear that she didn't understand what I was saying and that I was wrong. Once again, a wise man would have left it alone. A humble man wouldn't care about winning. I chose the foolish, arrogant route. I proceeded to send a fax over to her workplace diagramming the pace of a group of six versus the pace of two groups of three. I was immature. I made matters worse, but I won the argument.

Through the years, we've had arguments over Monopoly, Scrabble, Taboo, Settlers of Catan, the size of my brain, Mariah Carey, Santa Claus—you name it. We've also had more serious arguments about how to discipline our children, spend our money, and spend our time. We don't fight a ton, but we do fight. We are human, and we both love winning. I'm guessing we're not the only ones.

One verse that keeps us more grounded in this area than any other is James 4:6: "God opposes the proud, but gives grace to the humble."

For those of us who nurture a win-at-any-cost mentality, this verse should shake us to the core. Only a fool would sacrifice this much for any victory. Let this sink into your brain: God actively fights against the proud person. The pride required to win your argument and defeat your "enemy" provides you with a new opponent: God.

Can you imagine anything worse than fighting God? God fights for the humble. He pours out His grace upon the humble. We all love to win, but are we ready to give up the grace of God and take on His opposition? And once that happens, have you really won? Nothing is better than having God's grace lavished upon you, and nothing could be worse than facing God's opposition.

WHO DIED AND MADE YOU JESUS?

Every day, the world bombards you with messages of power, independence, and control. Jesus tells you the opposite: die to yourself.

> I have been crucified with Christ. It is no longer I
> who live, but Christ who lives in me. And the life
> I now live in the flesh I live by faith in the Son
> of God, who loved me and gave himself for me.
> (Galatians 2:20)

This isn't upper level, extra credit, AP Christianity. It's what we sign up for—to die to ourselves and become like Christ. In an effort to gain "converts," Christians often refrain from telling the full story. We want people to follow, so like cheap salesmen, we share the benefits without explaining the cost. We tell them about Jesus' promises of life and forgiveness, but we don't mention His calls for repentance and obedience. We avoid His promise that we will experience persecution. When we do this, we cheapen the gospel. The beauty of the gospel is that Christ is of such supreme worth that we would gladly sacrifice all to have Him. He is so beautiful that we would be fools to resist becoming like Him.

> Then Jesus told his disciples, "If anyone would come after me, let him deny himself and take up his cross and follow me. For whoever would save his life will lose it, but whoever loses his life for my sake will find it." (Matthew 16:24–25)

> But whatever gain I had, I counted as loss for the sake of Christ. Indeed, I count everything as loss because of the surpassing worth of knowing Christ Jesus my Lord. For his sake I have suffered the loss of all things and count them as rubbish, in order that I may gain Christ and be found in him, not having a righteousness of my own that comes from the law, but that which comes through faith in Christ, the righteousness from God that depends on faith—that I may know him and the power of his resurrection, and may share his sufferings, becoming like him in his death, that by any means possible I may attain the resurrection from the dead. (Philippians 3:8–11)

Baptism is meant to convey our death and burial with Christ. A Christian rises from the water in a picture of resurrection—brought up from the grave with a new life, a new identity (see Rom. 6:1–10). Your problem could be that you're not dead. You have never truly died to yourself. Picture your body hanging lifelessly on a cross. Paul states matter-of-factly that this is what happens to those who belong to Christ—"our old self was crucified with him" (Rom. 6:6). That is what we signed up for. We have told God that we no longer want to live for ourselves. We want Him to take over. We actually desire a Master. Unlike Adam and Eve in the garden, we want to submit to God's rule. We are happy to surrender. We are happy to see our life become His.

> For *you have died*, and your life is hidden with Christ in God. When *Christ who is your life* appears, then you also will appear with him in glory. (Colossians 3:3–4, emphasis added)

TRANSLATING JESUS

Years ago, I was preaching through an interpreter in Brazil. After one of my statements was translated, everyone burst into laughter. Normally that would be a good sign, but in this case, I hadn't said anything funny! Obviously something got twisted in the interpretation. And then a thought occurred to me: this translator could be saying *anything* right now, and I wouldn't know the difference. He could be putting his own words in my mouth, and I would never know!

Sometimes we can be like interpreters gone wild. Our whole job is to act like Christ and tell His message to the world, but we do and say our own thing instead. We are called to translate for God. We are supposed to represent Him and speak on His behalf.

> We are ambassadors for Christ, God making his appeal through us. We implore you on behalf of Christ, be reconciled to God. (2 Corinthians 5:20)

Rather than speaking in a thundering voice from the heavens, God chose to speak through us as His ambassadors. And He chose marriage as a billboard by which He could shout His message. So He calls us to cultivate marriages that represent Him accurately.

The most well-known passage on marriage is Ephesians 5. It is in this passage that the Apostle Paul explains how our marriage relationship should reflect the relationship between Christ and the church. It is also here that he describes our roles in marriage. There is some debate over these verses. There are those who take the descriptions of roles in marriage literally, and those who believe these commands were unique to their time and culture and no longer apply today.

Something I learned in seminary is that with every issue, there are two sides. And there are scholars on both sides who are more intelligent than I am. So the best I could do was to study, pray, examine my heart, and make a decision. My goal is to stand before God and be able to say, "I prayed and studied this passage. I tried to ignore my personal desires and interpreted it as best I could. I believed this is what it said, so I did my best to live by it." I also try to hold my views with humility, allowing God to convince me

of a better interpretation at any point in the future through more
study, prayer, and heart-examination.

As Lisa and I have studied this passage and the issues involved
over the years, our best understanding is to take these verses literally and to live it out just as it is written. We conclude that God
has called men to lead humbly and serve their wives sacrificially.
They should help their wives prepare for the moment she sees God.
We believe that God has called women to follow their husbands
and encourage them in their pursuit of Him.

We view obedience to these commands as a unique opportunity to show the world how wonderful it can be to follow godly
leadership. We live in a time when most people distrust and dislike
authority, and it spills over into an unwillingness to submit to
the lordship of Jesus. I often wonder how much of that is a direct
result of the ugliness of so many "Christian" marriages. And I
also wonder if that would change if our marriages were beautiful
portrayals of this passage.

> Wives, submit to your own husbands, as to the
> Lord. For the husband is the head of the wife even
> as Christ is the head of the church, his body, and
> is himself its Savior. Now as the church submits
> to Christ, so also wives should submit in every-
> thing to their husbands.

> Husbands, love your wives, as Christ loved the
> church and gave himself up for her, that he might
> sanctify her, having cleansed her by the washing

of water with the word, so that he might present the church to himself in splendor, without spot or wrinkle or any such thing, that she might be holy and without blemish. In the same way husbands should love their wives as their own bodies. He who loves his wife loves himself. For no one ever hated his own flesh, but nourishes and cherishes it, just as Christ does the church, because we are members of his body. "Therefore a man shall leave his father and mother and hold fast to his wife, and the two shall become one flesh." This mystery is profound, and I am saying that it refers to Christ and the church. However, let each one of you love his wife as himself, and let the wife see that she respects her husband. (Ephesians 5:22–33)

This passage speaks to both husbands and wives. I'll start by walking through those sections that speak to the men, then Lisa will address the sections that speak to the women.

LOVE LIKE A MAN

Husbands, love your wives. How? *As Christ loved the church and gave himself up for her.* I have been given a tremendous task. I am supposed to be Jesus. My love should remind Lisa of Christ's love. The longer life goes on, the more she should feel like she is married to Jesus. I should be so selfless that it reminds her of the cross. I should have such a high standard of purity that she never has reason to doubt my faithfulness. Just as she would never dream of being lied to by Jesus, she should be confident that I will never waver from the vow I made to her.

I have had several women tell me through the years that when they look at the roles given to husbands and wives in the Bible, the role of the man is much easier. Really? Are you reading the same passages I'm reading? I understand that Paul's instructions for wives are difficult to follow. But the command to love *in the same way that Christ loved* is not exactly a cakewalk. Our roles seem equally impossible. Thank God for His Spirit.

The Bible tells men to love their wives *as Christ loved the church.* Think about that. Jesus did not sit in heaven talking about His feelings for you. His love went way beyond words and feelings. Jesus was all about action. All about sacrifice. Way before you were even born He has been pursuing you—aggressively! He left the glory and comforts of heaven for you. He endured torture and ridicule for you. He endured the Father's wrath for you. No one will ever love you that much nor endure that much pain for you. He didn't sit passively in heaven criticizing you. He zealously came after you.

And He tells husbands simply to follow His example.

We cannot display Christ's love without hurting. Jesus "gave himself" for the church. This speaks of His death. There was nothing He withheld from His bride.

Even as I write this, I am struck by how short I fall of this standard. I am trying to imagine what it would look like if I actually lived this out. While some things seem to get easier in the Christian life, this one does not. At times I doubt whether I will ever be consistently selfless and sacrificial. It requires a moment by moment dying to myself. Jesus' standard is absolutely superhuman, and commands like Ephesians 5:25 can feel overwhelming.

This is why I have to constantly remind myself of the power of the Spirit. The call requires superhuman strength, and that is exactly what God has provided to us through the Holy Spirit.

Part of the problem is that so much of my sacrifice for my wife seems trivial compared to the cross: changing diapers, doing chores, eating food she likes—these things feel insignificant in comparison. It's embarrassing that I even struggle to do these things! In a sense, the bigger things seem easier, like taking a bullet for her. Or pushing her away from a speeding train (since Lisa is always playing on train tracks). Maybe I could muster up the courage for one glorious moment of sacrifice. But I need to look at the bigger picture. It's not just about making sacrifices, big or small. It's about character. It's about letting go of myself and constantly thinking of others. It's about becoming like Christ.

We have to remember why Christ made the sacrifice He did:

> ... that he might sanctify her, having cleansed her by the washing of water with the word, so that he might present the church to himself in splendor, without spot or wrinkle or any such thing, that she might be holy and without blemish. (Eph. 5:26–27)

Why did Jesus sacrifice Himself for the church? He was preparing us to meet God. Without His sacrifice, it would have been a horrifying encounter. God would have taken one look at our sinfulness and sent us to a terrifying end. But Jesus changed all of that. He sacrificed so we could stand before Him "holy and without blemish." It was the most loving thing He could have done.

If you are to love like Christ, then you also must concern yourself with your wife's sanctification.

Though Jesus has already taken all of her sin on the cross, you still have a real responsibility. You are to love, lead, and sacrifice in such a way that it results in your wife's sanctification. The most loving thing you can do is to lead your wife to be closer to Jesus, to become more like Him.

Practically speaking, this will mean encouraging her in her time alone with God. Sacrifice to make sure she has time. It will mean reminding her not to love the world or the things of the world. Keep her focus eternal. It will mean guiding her towards acts of love that will result in eternal reward. Men, have you ever considered your role as a husband in these terms? This is huge.

NEED MOTIVATION?

I am a very self-centered person. There are days when it feels like I can't stop thinking about myself. Intriguingly, Ephesians 5 explains how we can use this to our advantage. Paul tells us to love our wives as our own bodies (vv. 28–29). We don't have to remind ourselves to "nourish and cherish" our bodies. We do this naturally. Paul's analogy simply tells us to see our wives as an extension of ourselves.

Then Paul makes a fascinating statement. It is so shocking and unbelievable that I'm still praying that God would give me the faith to believe this wholeheartedly. Follow the logic in this passage:

> In the same way husbands should love their wives as their own bodies. He who loves his wife loves himself. For no one ever hated his own flesh, but nourishes and cherishes it, just as Christ does the church, because we are members of his body. (Ephesians 5:28–30)

Why should husbands love their wives as their own bodies? Because that is what Christ does for us. He "nourishes and cherishes" us "*because we are members of his body.*" Don't miss that! Jesus cares for me like I care for my own body! Soak that in. Do you believe it? Do you believe the Son of God cares for you like a member of His body? You should be overwhelmed with joy right now! Take some time to dwell on this and to thank God for this amazing truth.

When we deeply believe these truths and meditate on them, we begin to understand why David said, "The Lord is my Shepherd, *I shall not want*" (Psalm 23:1, emphasis added). David was not needy. And we shouldn't be either. Nothing is worse than a needy husband. If Jesus cares for us as members of His own body, what more could we ask for? This is why David says, "my cup overflows" (Psalm 23:5).

Are you needy? Or overflowing? When we meditate on all of the riches we have in Christ, we can't contain it all. Picture a Thanksgiving meal where you have eaten so much, you can't eat another bite. You beg everyone else to keep eating the leftovers because you have way too much. This is how our lives should look. We are filled in Christ. Beyond filled. Overflowing. So we turn to the people around us and share the abundance of love, peace, joy, and life.

Here's a blueprint for marriage:

1. We become overwhelmed by Christ's care for us.

2. So we shower our wives with the same love we receive from God.

3. Then, people are shocked by our extravagant love toward our wives.

4. As a result, we are given an opportunity to tell them about the love of Christ that compels us.

Sadly, very few marriages work this way. People rarely marvel when they observe Christian marriages. We only shock through our mediocrity. I suppose it should be surprising to watch someone claim to have the Spirit of God dwelling in them yet live an ordinary life.

But this can all change. It starts with you rejoicing about being a member of Christ's body.

Rejoice in the Lord always; again I will say, rejoice. (Philippians 4:4)

Take time to rejoice in Christ. Seriously. No woman wants to be led by a joyless man. Let Christ fill you so you have plenty to give your wife. Find all of your security and worth in being a child of God, a member of Christ's body. He "nourishes and cherishes" you, which enables you to do the same for your wife.

This has to be our motivation. It's your joy in Him that ought to motivate you to follow His example. Think about Jesus washing the feet of the disciples and then telling them to do that for one another. He didn't ask them to wash His feet, but one another's. As Jesus cares for you, you are to care for your wife.

MARRIAGE & HUMILITY —Lisa

Humility is so beautiful, isn't it? And yet so elusive. Because we love ourselves so very much, it's a struggle to consider others *more important than ourselves* (Phil. 2:3).

One day I decided to pay attention to all of those times I felt fighting feelings rising up inside. You know the feeling you get when someone offends you, cuts you off, takes too long, doesn't say "excuse me" or "thank you," short changes you, or is rude in some other way. I kept track of how many times these feelings flared up inside, and it was eye opening. It is a *fight* to choose humility, to actually be *clothed* in humility.

> I therefore, a prisoner for the Lord, urge you to walk in a manner worthy of the calling to which you have been called, *with all humility* and gentleness, with patience, bearing with one another in

love, eager to maintain the unity of the Spirit in the
bond of peace. (Ephesians 4:1–3, emphasis added)

Clothe yourselves, all of you, *with humility* toward
one another, for "God opposes the proud but gives
grace to the humble." (1 Peter 5:5, emphasis added)

This is radically different than what we've ever felt like doing.
This is radically different from the world's way of thinking. You're
not going to find any magazines on the newsstands with articles
encouraging you to show humility. Instead, we are saturated
with messages about power, independence, and control. We are
bombarded with advice telling us to listen to our own hearts, to
do whatever we feel like doing. The constant affirmation of the
world and the pull of our own hearts make it so easy to believe
that we deserve to be treated in a certain way. We should not have
to listen to anyone telling us what to do; after all, we are strong
and independent.

It scares me how easy it is to start thinking like the world
without realizing it. It troubles me that the majority of what we
pour into our minds is so worldly. Our thinking can stray so far
from biblical truth! Think about how much time you spend in a
normal week watching television and movies, reading magazines,
scrolling through the internet, and engaged in social media. Now
compare that with the amount of time you spend in the word of
God and in prayer. Scary?

I'm not trying to conjure up guilty feelings that leave you
feeling defeated. But I do want to give a wake-up call. We *will*
struggle with a worldly mindset if we aren't careful to guard

against it. Have you ever come back from a camp or retreat on a spiritual high, only to find that it doesn't last once you're back in the "real world"? Why does this happen? Because suddenly your mind is bombarded by a culture that wants nothing to do with Jesus. You had been feeding your spiritual appetite, and now the world is taunting you to feed your fleshly appetite.

> Do not love the world or the things in the world. If anyone loves the world, the love of the Father is not in him. For all that is in the world—the desires of the flesh and the desires of the eyes and pride of life—is not from the Father but is from the world. (1 John 2:15–16)

> See to it that no one takes you captive by philosophy and empty deceit, according to human tradition, according to the elemental spirits of the world, and not according to Christ. (Colossians 2:8)

The Enemy is cunning. In the most subtle of takeovers, he lies to us about everything, and especially about what we "deserve." He wants us to think of ourselves so highly that a humble heart is something to be laughed at. All that worldly wisdom sounds deceitfully good.

Here is the simplest place to start in this war for our minds:

> Keep your heart with all vigilance, for from it flow the springs of life. (Proverbs 4:23)

If my desire is to display the humility of Christ, I need constant input from the Scriptures to do so. I am so weak that I <u>must</u> keep my eyes on His example, and pray constantly for the Spirit to enable me to live for Him.

There is a battle we have to face every single day. There are weapons we have to pick up and be ready to defend ourselves with—every single day. To live in this world and not allow ourselves to be bullied and enticed by a mindset that is not biblical, we have to be seriously engaged, and seriously on our guard.

> Be on your guard; stand firm in the faith; be courageous; be strong. (1 Corinthians 16:13, NIV)

> Beloved, I urge you as sojourners and exiles to abstain from the passions of the flesh, which wage war against your soul. (1 Peter 2:11)

If we don't acknowledge the constant battle and begin to fight diligently, pride will sink deeper into our already self-serving hearts and destroy our lives and our marriages.

I have counseled and spoken with many women in troubled marriages. Many times I have cried with them. And I can tell you that no matter how varied the circumstances were, no matter who was most at fault, no matter how utterly hopeless the situation seemed, these women always responded in one of two ways: in pride or in humility. They all showed emotion, cried, endured pain, and struggled deeply. But some of these women made a choice to respond in pride, and some battled their wills and responded in humility.

Prideful people are defensive, angry, blame-shifting, and focused on self. They consistently see that the problem lies not with them, but with everyone else. The gospel is not the focus; it is not the goal.

Humble people are broken over their own sin, more concerned with honoring God than arguing about what they deserve, and try—by the grace of God—to stay focused on the gospel and the goal.

I remember sitting across the table from my friend Reisha, whose marriage was a wreck. Her husband had betrayed her, and at one point had even packed up his things and left. It looked like he was finally going to come back and try to reconcile with her, and Reisha was struggling. She looked me right in the eyes and said, "I don't love him. My heart doesn't feel anything for him."

It was her next statement that shocked me: "But I do love God, and I will do whatever it takes because I love Him. Is that okay? To do this out of my love for God, and not for my husband?" Honestly, in that moment, I had a million thoughts swirling in my mind. The grace of God that had flooded Reisha's heart silenced me. I was completely moved by her intense desire to honor God and obey what she knew He was asking her to do. Her love for God made her willing to do anything, regardless of how she felt, and regardless of how many people told her she deserved "better."

And praise God, their marriage completely turned around. This was one of the first times I witnessed the power of humility, and it is undeniable. Seeing God move like that changes your perspective on things. How many times have people allowed their pride to stand in the way of something beautiful that God was about to do?

We need to remember at every moment that God stands actively against us when we are prideful (James 4:6). You may think you are digging your heels in against your spouse, but it's ultimately God you're opposing, and you're inviting His opposition in return.

God has always loved humility. Always. And He generously pours out His grace on those who are humble. View your arguments with your spouse in this light. It doesn't matter what he said or what he did. The question is whether you want to experience God's opposition or His grace. Is it more important for you to be right? Or to do what's right?

The other day I was talking with a friend who was struggling with pride. She said, "If I apologize or back down or show humility, it makes me feel like he won." Say what you will, that thought is more familiar to us than we'd care to admit. Meanwhile, she was miserable because she knew things were not right. She even recognized that this was distancing her from God. I encouraged her that ultimately, the surrender was to God Himself.

We all know that gut-wrenching moment when you feel like you literally can't form the words, "I'm sorry" with your mouth. Pride washes over your body and mind. There is only one thing that will possess you to do what's right in that moment: an overwhelming need to be right with God. What else matters? I would go so far as to say that if this is still not motivation enough to swallow your pride, maybe it's time to look long and hard at your relationship with God.

> One's pride will bring him low,
>   but he who is lowly in spirit will obtain honor.
> (Proverbs 29:23)

This is the one to whom I will look:
> he who is humble and contrite in spirit
> and trembles at my word. (Isaiah 66:2)

Pride goes before destruction,
> and a haughty spirit before a fall. (Proverbs 16:18)

Toward the scorners he is scornful,
> but to the humble he gives favor. (Proverbs 3:34)

For though the LORD is high, he regards the lowly,
> but the haughty he knows from afar. (Psalm 138:6)

When I see someone showing humility, I point it out to my kids: "Isn't that so attractive?" I want them to recognize it. I want them to learn from it. I want them to realize that God has always said that humility is beautiful. I also want them to understand that when we act in humility, we are following Jesus' example.

So many marriages crumble because humility is lacking. As believers, isn't that a little sad? We strive for control and equality, caught up in a power struggle rather than the humble self-sacrifice of Christ.

So many women focus on what submission *does not* mean, and they never embrace what it *does* mean.

For many years, I taught a class for wives at our church on what it means to be a godly wife. It took me a long time, but I eventually realized that if we were truly humble people, we wouldn't need a class like that. That maybe we were over-thinking the wife part, and under-thinking who Christ calls us all to be in light of His example. Underneath every struggle and every discussion was this subtle realization that being like Christ would solve a whole lot of our problems.

There are healthy discussions to be had on the subject of roles in marriage. We obviously want to understand what the Bible is saying as clearly as possible. I don't want to circumvent those discussions, but this is how I like to think of it as a wife: there is no better way to stand apart from non-believers than in the way we respectfully submit to our husbands. We display our trust in Christ and God's word powerfully when we embrace His instruction to "submit to our husbands, as to the Lord." Without question, this is countercultural in America. But the reality is, if we truly desire to follow Jesus, we will definitely not fit in with this culture.

Here are a few good principles for thinking through the call to submission:

1. When we submit, we are respectfully submitting to a God-given *position*, and not *perfection*. In other words, our husbands are going to make mistakes. They will not always "deserve" to be the leader in our eyes, but God will always deserve our obedience to Him in this way. And since the command to submit comes from God, our submission is ultimately to Him.

2. Only our submission to God should be absolute. We are not meant to submit to our husbands if

they ask us to sin (get drunk, lie, cheat on taxes, watch pornography, etc.). "We must obey God rather than human beings!" (Acts 5:29, NIV).

3. We are designed to help our husbands, and to accomplish so much more *together!* God decided that it was "not good" for the man to be alone, so He created a helper fit for Adam (Gen. 2:18). Embrace your God-given role. Give your husband the benefit of your insight, wisdom, and perspective. But also give him the freedom to move and lead in the direction he feels God is leading.

4. There is no safer place to be than in the will of God. If we know God has asked us to submit to our husbands, we follow God in that, even though we may be fearful. Ultimately, more women find themselves fighting against God rather than their husbands. And that's a big reason why so many women are completely miserable. God has carefully crafted every aspect of marriage, and we need to learn to trust Him.

5. The biblical concept of submission does not put your husband in the place of God. If a woman finds herself being subjected to abuse, she shouldn't hesitate to involve the authorities that can hold her husband accountable. But I also want to encourage

every wife to believe that God can bring resto-
ration and healing in even the most hopeless of
situations.

Ultimately, we entrust ourselves to God.

It's pretty astounding that Jesus Himself willingly submitted to
the Father in order to accomplish His purposes. When I am tempted
to complain or wonder why women are given the role of submission,
I'm reminded that our Savior Himself said, "I do nothing on my
own authority" (John 8:28) and "I have come down from heaven,
not to do my own will but the will of him who sent me" (John 6:38).

Submission is beautiful when we realize we are imitating Christ.
Though He rightfully possessed all glory, He willingly laid it aside
(Phil. 2). If anyone *deserved* to be treated a certain way, it was Him.
And yet He gladly placed Himself in submission to the Father.
Amazing! Take your eyes off of the world long enough to let the
truths of Scripture take root in your heart.

All that said, I truly believe that our roles in marriage should be
de-emphasized in light of the most pressing calling of all believers
to be Christ-like. Remember that we are all commanded to be
humble (1 Pet. 5:5–6) and we are all commanded to submit to one
another (Eph. 5:21), because Jesus personified these characteristics.
The more you grow in your pursuit of Christ-likeness, the more
you will naturally live out your God-given role.

Do nothing from selfish ambition or conceit, but
in humility count others more significant than
yourselves. (Philippians 2:3)

How are you doing with this? Would anyone who knows you well be quick to describe you as humble?

CONCLUSION

Beautiful people make beautiful marriages. Jesus is the most beautiful person to ever walk the earth. Your best shot at having a beautiful marriage is if both of you make it your goal to become like Jesus. While husbands are told specifically to love like Christ loved, Jesus is the standard for every believer.

> "A new commandment I give to you, that you love one another: just as I have loved you, you also are to love one another. By this all people will know that you are my disciples, if you have love for one another." (John 13:34–35)

When we both make it our goal to love each other with the love of Christ, the conflicts we have regarding roles and responsibilities dissipate. If I am earnestly seeking Lisa's good before my own, I don't find it insulting or even inconvenient that I am supposed to serve her and sacrifice on her behalf. It's just obvious. It's natural. And if Lisa cares for me above herself, it is obvious she would want to support my vision for ministry and life above her own. Imagine a marriage—or any relationship, for that matter—where both parties are trying desperately to "outdo one another in showing honor" (Rom. 12:10).

As we know, being like Jesus is much easier said than done. Becoming like Him depends on being with Him. Stay close to Him.

Rejoice in Him, and allow Him to cherish and nourish you as a member of His body.

Many of us are problem solvers, and we approach every aspect of our lives with that mentality. Even in our prayers we jump in with requests, taking no time to just enjoy His presence and blessings. Life gets busy, and intimacy with Christ gets sacrificed. We get focused on tasks and neglect character development. My zeal for accomplishing much crowds out my need to love much. I need to be close to Jesus, recognizing His presence with me, praising Him throughout the day.

Practicing His presence helps me tremendously. Right now, I picture Him sitting across from me. He is strong, fearless, loving, pure, and humble. He gives life wherever He goes. I need that constant awareness of His presence. I need to always be drawing closer to Him. I need to always ask Him to make me more like Himself.

Wherever you are right now, picture Christ sitting across from you. Think of how He would be acting. Picture His boldness and His humility. Imagine His power and grace. Try to think of the selfless acts He would be performing if He dwelt in the flesh today. Now ask for the ability to walk in His footsteps. Ask Jesus to live through you. To love through you.

Take action by truly *loving* your spouse—not only through words, but showing love in the way Jesus showed love. Unless the Bible is wrong, we have been given the ability to walk like Jesus. We have to keep believing this. We have to keep striving for this as we eagerly await His return.

DO SOMETHING

Everything we've discussed in this section is vitally important for marriage, life, and your relationship with God. But concepts like humility and self-sacrifice are notoriously difficult to put into practice. You should really spend the rest of your life and the rest of your marriage trying to live more humbly and more sacrificially with respect to the people around you. Use the suggestions below to get you started on this process, but don't stop there. Continue to find more and more ways to practically love your spouse.

TAKE A LONG LOOK AT JESUS.

+ *Spend some time thinking about Jesus. Don't rush this. What do you find compelling about Him? What makes Him so beautiful? What characteristics does He embody that you are drawn to? What actions did He perform that grab your attention?*

+ *After considering this for a while, make a list. What is it that makes Jesus so compelling?*

+ *Share your thoughts with your spouse. What did your spouse notice that you didn't?*

+ *Have an honest conversation about what each of you would look like if you were to imitate these qualities of Jesus in your marriage. Be very practical in your descriptions.*

EVALUATE YOUR CHRIST-LIKENESS.

✦ *Sit down with a piece of paper and make a list of areas where you believe you are demonstrating Christ-likeness. This doesn't mean you're perfect in these areas, just put down ways in which you are seeing some resemblance to Jesus.*

✦ *Next, make a list of areas in which you need to grow in your Christ-likeness. Be honest.*

✦ *Share your lists with each other. Don't use this as an opportunity to sink in those criticisms you've been too fearful to share; rather, let this be an honest conversation about the ways in which you do and don't resemble Christ. Since we all have blind spots, it's helpful to get your spouse's input on where you are actually doing well, and where you most need to grow.*

✦ *Discuss ways in which you can help each other in this journey towards Christ-likeness.*

✦ *Begin and end this time prayerfully, asking God to draw you together as you seek to become more like Him.*

Don't Waste Your Marriage

MARRIAGE IN LIGHT OF OUR MISSION

When my daughter Mercy was five, she joined a soccer team. She looked adorable in her bright blue uniform. She was a part of the "Blue Lightning." As a pretty competitive dad, I had visions of my daughter stealing the ball from the opposing team, scoring goals, and winning. So I didn't know whether to laugh or scream when I watched Mercy and her friend holding hands, skipping along the field, and picking flowers while the game was going on. I think I did a little of both. It was obvious that she didn't care about winning. She just wanted to have fun. But as her dad, my question was: If all she wanted to do was pick flowers, then why was I paying for her to be on a soccer team? I guess it was to get some cute pictures in her uniform.

So many couples act like five-year-old soccer players when it comes to the spiritual war that we find ourselves in. God calls us to fight in an ongoing battle against darkness. In this battle,

He has given us a clear mission—to make disciples. Yet Christian couples can most typically be found holding hands and skipping through life, ignoring the battle that rages around them. We have made happy families our mission. That is not the mission that Jesus gave us, but we try to justify this idolizing of marriage because *it's what we want.*

As we have been saying, marriage is important, but it's not most important. When we focus on what is most important, our marriages will thrive because they will be functioning according to their design. But if we focus too intently on our families, we will actually fail at life, and therefore at marriage.

> Share in suffering as a good soldier of Christ Jesus. No soldier gets entangled in civilian pursuits, since his aim is to please the one who enlisted him. (2 Timothy 2:3–4)

The Bible teaches that we are at war. It is a real war with a very real enemy (2 Cor. 10:3–4, Eph. 6:10–20). God has given us a mission, so we cannot allow ourselves to "get entangled in civilian pursuits."

Picture a nice house with a white picket fence and your happy family lounging inside. Now imagine a full-scale war unfolding just a few blocks away. Your friends and neighbors are fighting for their lives while you are remodeling your kitchen and hanging your new big screen TV. You have contractors installing better windows so you can tune out all of the noise.

It is a pretty pathetic picture, but it's an appropriate comparison for the lives that so many Christian couples have chosen. They are ignoring Jesus' mission in hopes of enjoying life. Don't fall for it. Real life is found in the battle. Right now, we have many brothers and sisters being tortured overseas because of their faith. Let's pray for them and be encouraged by their example to enter the fight.

> "For whoever would save his life will lose it, but whoever loses his life for my sake and the gospel's will save it." (Mark 8:35)

As we mentioned earlier, part of the mission is having a healthy marriage. Our mission does not call us to neglect our marriages. But a marriage cannot be healthy unless we are seeking His kingdom and righteousness *first* (Matt. 6:33). Being in war together is what keeps us from being at war with each other. For those who have the Spirit in them, there is a longing to be in the battle. We want to be used. We want to be a part of His mission.

In this chapter, we are going to call you to seek the kingdom before your marriage. We are going to challenge you to spend your life on the battlefield. Specifically, we will explore eight reasons to center your marriage around His mission.

8 REASONS TO FOCUS ON THE MISSION

1. Jesus commanded it.

This should be all the reason we need. Our Master gave us a command. In fact, it was the last thing He said before ascending back into Heaven.

> And Jesus came and said to them, "All authority
> in heaven and on earth has been given to me. Go
> therefore and make disciples of all nations, baptiz-
> ing them in the name of the Father and of the Son
> and of the Holy Spirit, teaching them to observe
> all that I have commanded you. And behold, I am
> with you always, to the end of the age." (Matthew
> 28:18–20)

Though all of Jesus' commands should be taken seriously,
the setting of this command adds some additional weight. Jesus
rose from the dead, gathered His followers, and explained that *all
authority on heaven and earth* had been given to Him! Can you
imagine a more dramatic setting? Ignoring the one command that
the newly resurrected King of the Universe delivered to you could
certainly qualify as the stupidest thing you could do in your lifetime.

So what's the command? Make disciples. Our lives should
revolve around these two words. Whether as individuals or as
couples, our mission is to make as many disciples as we can during
our time on earth. This takes priority over everything else. So
assuming you haven't done so already, you should sit down with your
spouse tonight and figure out how to structure your lives around
the command to make disciples. This command should dictate
everything about your life: where you live, where you work, where
you spend your money, how you spend your time—everything!
You should not make a single decision without the words "make
disciples" factoring in. We should be constantly asking ourselves

the question: How can we free up more time and resources for making disciples?

I want us all to be clear on what this means. Jesus was telling His followers to go to those who did not know about Him. They were to reach people who didn't have a relationship with Him. They were to baptize them and teach them to obey His commands.

Jesus is calling for more than Bible studies. He wants us living life with others so we can demonstrate a life of obedience and teach them to do the same (1 Cor. 11:1). True discipleship involves opening up our homes, schedules, and resources to others in order to allow them to see Christ and follow Him.

You exist to make disciples. Your marriage exists to make disciples. You don't want to stand before God at the end of your life with no disciples. Restructure your life. Re-prioritize. You exist to influence others.

So much more needs to be said on this topic. I encourage you to go to multiplymovement.com and spend some time working through the free material that I've compiled there on the subject of making disciples.

2. Jesus is on the battlefield.

Jesus makes an astounding promise at the end of His great commission. After telling us to go throughout the world making disciples, He promises to accompany us. We are not working alone.

> "And behold, I am with you always, to the end of the age." (Matthew 28:20)

God is currently on a mission. He is redeeming the earth. If I want to find my friend Andrew, I can usually find him at the gym. If I want to find Adam, he's probably at the beach. If I want to find Lisa, she's probably at Target. If I want to find Jesus, I should share the gospel with someone. That's where He will be. He is on the battlefield. He is pursuing the mission.

I hear people complain that they don't feel Jesus with them, they don't experience the Holy Spirit. I usually ask them: Are you busy making disciples? After all, His promise came on the heels of His command. Later, Jesus told His disciples that they would receive power when the Holy Spirit came upon them. But that power was given so they could be His "witnesses."

> "But you will receive power when the Holy Spirit has come upon you, and you will be my witnesses in Jerusalem and in all Judea and Samaria, and to the end of the earth." (Acts 1:8)

Jesus was not giving us His Spirit so that we could merely feel Him, like some kind of divine teddy bear. He gave us the Spirit and His power so we could be His witnesses. And He accompanies us, not so we can have happy families, but so we can make disciples. It is true that we can experience Him by praying on a mountaintop or worshiping Him with other believers. But there is a special way that He shows up when we are on His battlefield.

My daughter had a concert one night, and I was scheduled to speak afterwards. During the concert, I was backstage, on my knees, begging God to move. I was praying to the point of frustration. It went something like this:

> *"Lord, please do something while I preach! You know*
> *I ask for this all the time! I want to see you move.*
> *You tell me in Scripture that Elijah was merely a*
> *man, just like me, yet you moved when he prayed.*
> *You sent fire from heaven and moved the crowd to*
> *fear and worship. Show yourself as I proclaim your*
> *truth! Why don't you answer? Why won't you do the*
> *same thing for me?"*

While I didn't hear an audible voice, it was one of those rare occasions where I believe the Lord gave me an answer at that moment. It went something like this:

> *"Elijah was on Mount Carmel battling prophets of*
> *Baal. If I hadn't sent fire from heaven, he would have*
> *been beheaded. You…are at a Christian concert."*

Then I was reminded of so many of the stories I love in Scripture. Throughout the Bible, God appeared powerfully when His followers took risks for His sake. God made His presence and power obvious when Elijah called hundreds of pagan prophets to recognize the One True God (1 Kings 18). When Shadrach, Meshach, and Abednego refused to bow to the King's idol, they were thrown into a super-heated furnace only to find another

Person standing beside them and delivering them from the flames (Dan. 3). When Stephen was about to be stoned to death for proclaiming Christ, he saw Jesus!

> Now when they heard these things they were enraged, and they ground their teeth at him. But he, full of the Holy Spirit, gazed into heaven and saw the glory of God, and Jesus standing at the right hand of God. And he said, "Behold, I see the heavens opened, and the Son of Man standing at the right hand of God." (Acts 7:54–56)

God has a pattern of showing up mysteriously and powerfully on the battlefield.

My greatest moments on earth have been the times when I experienced firsthand the supernatural work of God. I have been moved to tears, trembling, and awe. There is nothing greater than experiencing God. Human relationships can be good, but nothing compares to a human being encountering God. Get in the battle, take some risks, and you will experience Him too.

3. People are dying.

In the time it took you to read this sentence, four people died. On average, two people die every second. That's 155,000 every day, and very few of them are going to heaven (Matt. 7:13–14). For me, that's depressing. Overwhelming. The only way to escape the pain of this truth is to deny or ignore it.

The Apostle Paul speaks of living with "great sorrow and unceasing anguish" (Rom. 9:2). Think of the intensity of those terms. Unceasing anguish? He knew the destiny of those who didn't trust Jesus, and that knowledge pained him deeply. The book of Acts records his efforts to reach everyone he could despite the severe costs. His life reflected his beliefs. While many of us would say we believe what Paul believed, our lives do not reflect it.

If we believe that billions are dying and heading for God's judgment, does it really make sense to center our lives around anything other than the mission to reach them? Don't be paralyzed by the numbers. Just do your part. You probably won't make a big dent in that number, but you will have an eternal impact on the lives of those that you do reach.

When I was a kid, my youth pastor asked: "If everyone in the youth group was just like you, what kind of youth group would we have?" It's a great way to think about our responsibility. Obviously, we are all unique, and each of us has a different gift. But you get the point. If every believer shared the gospel as often as you, how many would be reached? If everyone gave the percentage of their income you did, how much would we have to give to the poor?

Do you need stats on how many kids are homeless, enslaved, trafficked, raped, or starving to death at this moment? If so, just Google it. There is a lot of work to be done. Many are in desperate need—spiritually and physically. We can't ignore their cries. Sometimes I picture myself panicking in Africa with my family desperate for food and water, and I imagine what my attitude would be towards "Christians" in America. What would I feel if

I saw the way they lived and heard how they complained about not having enough?

Imagine right now a family of four living in India. They used to be a family of five, but they sold one of the daughters into slavery so the rest of the family could survive another month. Imagine them watching the daily routine of your family. What would they think of your Christian love?

The second greatest commandment, Jesus said, is to love your neighbor as yourself. Have you even loved your next-door neighbor like this, let alone your neighbors in Africa and India? Remember, Jesus referred to this as the most important thing you can do after loving God (Mark 12:31).

> By this we know love, that he laid down his life for us, and we ought to lay down our lives for the brothers. But if anyone has the world's goods and sees his brother in need, yet closes his heart against him, how does God's love abide in him? Little children, let us not love in word or talk but in deed and in truth. (1 John 3:16–18)

Consider this testimony from a Christian man who lived in Germany during the Holocaust:

> "We heard stories of what was happening to Jews, but we were trying to distance ourselves from it because what could we do to stop it? A railroad track ran behind our small church, and each

Sunday morning we could hear the whistle in the distance and the wheels coming over the tracks. We became disturbed when we heard the cries coming from the train as it passed by. We realized it was carrying Jews like cattle in the cars.

"Week after week, the whistle would blow. We dreaded to hear the sound of those wheels because we knew that we would hear the cries of the Jews en route to a death camp. Their screams tormented us. We knew the time the train was coming. And when we heard the whistle blow, we began singing hymns. By the time the train passed our church, we were singing at the top of our voices. If we heard the screams, we were singing more loudly. And soon we could hear them no more.

"Although years have passed, I still hear the train whistle in my sleep. God forgive me. Forgive all of us who call themselves Christians and yet did nothing to intervene."[2]

It's easy to be judgmental when you hear that story. It is sickening that Christians could hear their cries and drown them out by singing hymns. But what would you have done? Look at the pattern of your life. Would you really have gone against the norm and done something? If everyone else was singing, wouldn't you have just sung along?

Based on the patterns in my life, I can't say for sure what I would have done. But I know the kind of man I would like to be. Don't we all want to be the kind of people who are willing to stand up and say, "I can't live like this anymore! I can't follow the trend and pretend that nothing is happening!"

It's easy to look at other moments in history and criticize the church for their poor response. The difficult part is looking at the world right now and assessing your response. Does your marriage make sense in light of the existence of hell? Does your use of time and money make sense in light of the suffering in the world today?

4. You were created for this mission.

God made you for a reason. Like a toaster, stoplight, or aircraft carrier, you were designed a specific way for a specific purpose.

> For we are his workmanship, created in Christ Jesus
> for good works, which God prepared beforehand,
> that we should walk in them. (Ephesians 2:10)

God set this course for you "beforehand." God told the prophet Jeremiah that his course was set even before he was born:

> "Before I formed you in the womb I knew you,
>   and before you were born I consecrated you;
> I appointed you a prophet to the nations."
>   (Jeremiah 1:5)

You are different than everyone else on earth for a reason. And you have a supernatural gift to offer the church. To say that you are useless or ungifted is to say that God failed.

> To each is given the manifestation of the Spirit for the common good… All these are empowered by one and the same Spirit, who apportions to each one individually as he wills. (1 Corinthians 12:7, 11)

I used to think that I was being humble by making statements like, "I'm not very gifted. I'm just an average guy who isn't great at anything." A deeper study of Scripture convinced me that this wasn't humility, but a lack of faith. The HOLY SPIRIT OF GOD is empowering me! Why would I be self-deprecating? If Christ is living through me and the Spirit of God is empowering me, shouldn't I be powerful? Don't let the enemy tell you anything different. If you are a follower of Christ, you are filled with divine power. The Spirit of God unleashes His power when you use your gift for the good of the church body.

I'm usually so joyful when I get done teaching. There is a unique communion I experience with the Holy Spirit when I am using my gift to build up the church. It is the reason for my existence.

We have all gone through periods in life when we've thought, *this can't be all there is.* You feel trapped in meaningless routine and everything in you knows you were created for more. Life might be fun and relationships might be good, but you know something deeper is missing. You sense that you were created for more. You want to experience a deeper communion with God where the supernatural power of the Holy Spirit is flowing through you undeniably. You want to touch God rather than merely talk about Him.

You long for a knowledge of God that goes beyond your intellect, the kind of deep knowledge that only comes from experience. This happens only when you are on His mission. His love and power flow through you to others as you seek to bring them into His kingdom. There is nothing like it, and there's no other way to get it.

The older you get, the more panicked you can become. You look back at how seldom you experienced God and how little you have done for the kingdom. You then become hesitant to face God, knowing that you spent your time and money on yourself. I've seen people come to this overwhelming realization and become depressed or paralyzed. That is not what God wants. He wants a generation of elderly people who are willing to change, even though they are told they cannot. The younger generation needs the example of older men and women who are willing to repent. Willing to admit that they have lived their lives selfishly rather than for the kingdom. Eager to change their ways and now live for eternity. Motivated to warn younger believers not to repeat their mistakes.

The way it's supposed to work is that the older you become, the more excited you become. You should be able to look back at life and know that you accomplished what you were put on earth to do. This is exactly what Jesus was able to say: "I glorified you on earth, having accomplished the work that you gave me to do" (John 17:4).

And Paul must have been ecstatic when he wrote the following words to Timothy. Can you imagine being able to say this one day?

> As for you, always be sober-minded, endure suffering, do the work of an evangelist, fulfill your ministry. For I am already being poured out as a drink offering, and the time of my departure has come. I have fought the good fight, I have finished the race, I have kept the faith. Henceforth there is laid up for me the crown of righteousness, which the Lord, the righteous judge, will award to me on that Day, and not only to me but also to all who have loved his appearing. (2 Timothy 4:5–8)

He was telling young Timothy to stay focused on the mission no matter how painful it gets. As an older man, Paul assures him that it's worth it, because one day Timothy could be in the same position that he was in. Paul's life was coming to a close, and he knew that he finished the race. He did what he was supposed to do on the earth and was heading to heaven to collect his reward.

Try to imagine being in Paul's shoes at that point. Soak in the excitement. Paul followed Christ faithfully despite a bad start (1 Tim. 1:12–16). He fulfilled his mission on earth despite beatings, imprisonments, and temptations. Now he was nearing death and awaiting his reward. Who in their right mind would not want to trade places with Paul at that point? To be able to make a statement like this at the end of your life—what more could you want? Is your life heading in this direction?

5. The mission provides financial security.

Financial security is not a bad thing, but it depends on where you find your security. When most people speak of this, they are referring to having a large retirement account to rest in. When Jesus speaks of it, He refers to investing resources into the kingdom and trusting the Father to provide.

> "Do not be anxious, saying, 'What shall we eat?' or 'What shall we drink?' or 'What shall we wear?' For the Gentiles seek after all these things, and your heavenly Father knows that you need them all. But seek first the kingdom of God and his righteousness, and all these things will be added to you." (Matthew 6:31–33)

God promises that He is watching and is aware of your needs. And He promises that He will provide all of your needs *if* you seek His kingdom and His righteousness *first*. According to this promise, if I focus on furthering His kingdom, I am guaranteed my daily provisions.

The problem with this promise is that it's not enough for most of us. As Americans, we would be angry with God if He only provided our necessities. I have seen this played out over and over, where people question the existence of God because they only have slightly more than they need.

We live in a land of luxury. Our government already promises basic provisions; God's promise is currently unneeded in America. Though we may believe He would provide if the government does not, it is still a weak promise to us. We want Him to guarantee us a certain standard of living. We're not satisfied with a promise that He will meet our needs.

But for those who know contentment, this is a great promise. If you can say with Paul, "if we have food and clothing, with these we will be content" (1 Tim. 6:8), then you have nothing to worry about. Ever.

We know that if we seek His kingdom, we will be fine. God is aware of our needs, and He will meet them as He sees fit. We will eat, but may not be able to eat out. We will have clothes, but they may not match. We will have water, but it may not be bottled. For the content, this is a great promise. It takes all of the stress away. You never know what might happen to our country and economy, but the kingdom seeker is always secure.

I see so many building their own kingdoms. By doing so, you might have a larger home, nicer car, and better food on earth. Maybe. But you're on your own. You sacrifice knowing that God will provide for you regardless of what happens in our world. For those who seek His kingdom first, however, we never have to worry. Ever. God will always provide, and it is a rush to watch Him. For Lisa and I, some of our best memories have been the times when we watched God keep His promise.

6. This is the path to a happy marriage.

Truth be told, Lisa and I have very little in common. I love sports, she doesn't. She loves the mall, I hate it with a passion. She likes to sing, and I sound like a cow. I love weird Asian food, she thinks it's creepy. I love to surf, she won't go in the ocean. She likes serious conversations, I enjoy sarcasm. She loves Jesus. I love Jesus. And that's enough.

It is our mutual love for Jesus that binds us, and our love for His mission in particular. We both love helping people repent of their sin, turn to Jesus, and be filled with the Spirit. I love watching her share her faith, disciple younger women, care for the poor, and minister to children. This may sound weird, but watching her minister attracts me to her even more. And she loves it when I speak for God fearlessly, even when others hate it. She encourages me to minister and assures me that she will take good care of the kids while I'm out speaking and serving.

We love being on the mission *together*. In fact, it is the times when we neglect the mission and just focus on our own desires that conflict arises. Staying on the mission is what draws us closer together.

> Only let your manner of life be worthy of the gospel of Christ, so that whether I come and see you or am absent, I may hear of you that you are standing firm in one spirit, with one mind striving side by side for the faith of the gospel…
> (Philippians 1:17)

Paul's desire for the Philippians is our desire for our marriage. We want to be of "one mind," to be "striving side by side for the faith of the gospel." We work as a team and win as a team. Honestly, we don't spend much time working on our unity. The unity has come as a result of the mission. It has been a byproduct of serving the Lord.

If you have ever been on a short-term mission trip, you have probably experienced what I am talking about. Very often, you go with complete strangers. As you look around, you see that you have very little in common with the others on your trip. But by the time you leave, there is a bond between you. Your effort wasn't directed at building that bond. You were focused on the mission, but the mission brought you together.

Or think of a sports team embracing with joy after winning a championship. There is a temporary unity as long as they are focused on the same prize. They didn't hold hands and go through counseling to become better friends. They focused on the championship, and the bond formed naturally. The same is true with marriage and family.

Unity is the natural result of two people following one Spirit in a life devoted to the mission.

I have even seen marriages saved through a renewed focus on the mission. My friend Carl was counting down the days. Once his son graduated from high school and moved out, he was going to leave his wife. Unbeknown to Carl, his wife was thinking the same thing. After all, their son was the only thing they had in common. The love between them had been gone for a while. This is a common scenario. Couples can easily place all of their focus on their kids; once the kids are gone, so is the marriage.

But something happened with Carl's wife. She suddenly became obsessed with God's mission for her life. She developed a heart for girls caught up in the sex industry. She began seeking ways to rescue them from that life and exposing them to Jesus. She eventually started her own ministry of rescuing girls and helping to restore their lives. Her passion was so contagious that Carl couldn't help but serve with her. In his words, as he saw her compassion, she became attractive to him. As they embraced God's mission, they were united. Today, they clearly love each other and run this ministry together.

7. God's mission is bigger than your marriage.

Most would consider 1 Corinthians 7 the one chapter you would not include in a marriage book. After all, it speaks of being single. But it carries a vital lesson for married couples. Actually, this passage may have been more influential than any other in motivating us to write this book. It is in 1 Corinthians 7 that the same Paul who in Ephesians commanded husbands to love their wives tells us: "let those who have wives live as though they had none" (v. 29). What?

His point is that life on earth is short. There is an urgency to the period of time in which we live—after Jesus' resurrection and before His second coming. We all have callings from God, and those callings are bigger than our marriages. Seeking His kingdom must be our first priority, and if we're not careful, marriage can get in the way.

The appointed time has grown very short. From now on, let those who have wives live as though they had none, and those who mourn as though they were not mourning, and those who rejoice as though they were not rejoicing, and those who buy as though they had no goods, and those who deal with the world as though they had no dealings with it. For the present form of this world is passing away.

I want you to be free from anxieties. The unmarried man is anxious about the things of the Lord, how to please the Lord. But the married man is anxious about worldly things, how to please his wife, and his interests are divided. And the unmarried or betrothed woman is anxious about the things of the Lord, how to be holy in body and spirit. But the married woman is anxious about worldly things, how to please her husband. I say this for your own benefit, not to lay any restraint upon you, but to promote good order and to secure your undivided devotion to the Lord. (1 Corinthians 7:29–35)

That last verse is the key to the passage. It is the key to life. All of us are to pursue "undivided devotion to the Lord." We cannot allow marriage to distract us from the higher calling. In verse 34, he makes it clear that marriage can turn our eyes away from Jesus and toward each other in an unhealthy way. We end up seeking to please each other rather than pleasing Him. Marriage can bring us to a point where our "interests are divided" (v. 34), when our goal is actually an "undivided devotion to the Lord" (v. 35).

When things are good in marriage, we are tempted to enjoy each other more than Jesus. When things are bad, we can let our hurts in marriage distract us from loving Jesus. Lisa and I have many friends whose marriages are "good" by most definitions, but that seems to distract them from their mission. Can you really call your marriage "good" if your focus on your family keeps you from making disciples, caring for the poor, reaching out to the lost, and using your talents and resources for others? It is true that a healthy relationship is important for the sake of the mission, but we must be wary of enjoying marriage too much. Even good things can become idols (Rom. 1:25). The goal is "undivided devotion to the Lord." Don't let your affection or your disagreements distract you from His desires, His mission.

This is not to say that marriage is always a distraction. Paul explains that marriage can help the mission. For some, getting married actually frees us from distraction. Earlier in the passage Paul explains that in some cases, marriage can keep us from unnecessary sexual temptation (1 Cor. 7:1-5). Don't forget that marriage is a good thing. God designed it, after all. He established it in the Garden of Eden before sin entered the world. Indeed, marriage can enable us to do more than we could accomplish alone (Gen. 2:18-25).

But like every good thing, Satan can use our relationships with each other for evil. Sadly, we believe that this has become the norm in our churches. Marriage-centered marriages have become accepted and applauded rather than Christ-centered ones.

We often hear the phrase "God first, family second" in church circles. While we say it a lot, I don't see how this phrase is actually impacting anyone. Think about it. What if you were to switch to a "family first" mentality? What actions would you really have to change?

8. The return of Christ compels us.

I'm tempted to walk through Matthew 24–25 at this point, but it might be better if you just read those two chapters for yourself. Seriously, grab your Bible and read these two important chapters. Pray about them, read them, and come to your own conclusions about how the return of Jesus should affect our lives today.

TRAINING TO REACH THE GOAL —Lisa

Growing up, all I ever wanted to be was a wife and mom. My heart was set on marrying a Christian man (marrying a pastor did not cross my mind), and raising Christian children. Honestly, I didn't think very far beyond that. It wasn't a wrong desire; clearly God did not want me married to an unbeliever, and children have always been a blessing. But without even realizing it, I had elevated these roles higher than my truest identity as a child of God. Much of my effort went into being a great wife and mom, rather than being a great woman of God.

Honestly, I never really prayed and asked God what *He* wanted from me. I was on autopilot, blindly following my own assumptions about my purpose here on earth. Obviously God wants me to love my husband and train my children well. The danger comes in when we overemphasize *anything* other than the fact that we are here for His purposes.

You are more than a spouse. If you have been blessed with kids, you are more than a parent. You have a unique role in the kingdom of God, and He has great works for you to do that He planned before you were born.

> For we are his workmanship, created in Christ Jesus for good works, which God prepared beforehand, that we should walk in them. (Ephesians 2:10)

Read that verse for yourself a few times. Doesn't it seem crazy that we would not actively pursue whatever good works God planned from eternity past? It isn't like the universe is going to fall apart without you, but God has *invited* us into His kingdom work. *You* are the one missing out here. I know I was until I recognized that God had something bigger going on than my own little world.

I'm not trying to tell you to neglect your spouse or resent your children. No way. I'm asking you to consider a world outside of your Christian bubble. I'm sorry if that sounds harsh, but I was in that bubble! And when it popped, it may have startled me, but it has also freed me. For some of you, it isn't about the Christian bubble, it's just the plain old "idolatry" of the family. I want you to seriously ask yourself: Do I spend more time focusing on being a good spouse and parent, or more time focusing on being a godly person?

I'm talking about the difference between, "I'm taking the kids to the park today because they will love that" and "I'm inviting our new neighbor to the park with us because not only will my kids love it, I can reach out to her and make sure she knows I am here for her if she needs anything."

It's also the very simple but *profound* difference between running each day off your own agenda, and actually taking the time to be with Jesus, to pray and ask Him to show you the people He wants you to love and the needs He wants you to meet.

In a job, you would automatically understand that your objective is to accomplish the tasks your boss laid out for you. If you genuinely didn't know which tasks were most important or time-sensitive, you would find your boss and ask him.

As believers, Jesus is our Lord and Master, and yet we neglect many of the things He asks us to do. When this happens, Jesus asks, "Why do you call me 'Lord, Lord,' and not do what I tell you?" (Luke 6:46)

When I think about being on a mission, I get the picture of an athlete in my mind. I am probably one of the least athletic people you could find. But I have always *loved* to watch gymnastics and ice skating. (So girly, I know.) I often find myself thinking about everything these athletes go through to become so good at what they do. It's amazing! They are completely focused and dedicated. Listen to one of their interviews, and you will hear about the things they give up, the relationships they sacrifice, the time they pour into their sport! They live with one goal in mind. They are on a *mission*.

We need to live like this.

> Do you not know that in a race all the runners run,
> but only one receives the prize? So run that you
> may obtain it. Every athlete exercises self-control
> in all things. They do it to receive a perishable
> wreath, but we an imperishable. So I do not run
> aimlessly; I do not box as one beating the air. But
> I discipline my body and keep it under control,
> lest after preaching to others I myself should be
> disqualified. (1 Corinthians 9:24–27)

As Christians, we should be the most disciplined, eager, focused, loving people around. The mission is worth the training, the sacrifice, the pain. If we have one goal in mind, we will be willing to lay down our lives, and be ready to forsake everything for the mission that Christ calls us to.

We cannot afford to run around aimlessly, each doing our own thing. Each of us has a responsibility to honor God and run the race well, regardless of what everyone else is doing. But let's face it, marriage is a team effort. It will function best when both husband and wife are committed to the mission. When one person on the team is slacking, it throws everything off.

But here's where Paul's training analogy is so powerful. You may have to pull extra weight; you may have to work even harder. But when you are in the race, when you have the goal fixed in your mind, you do what it takes. Because even though it's unfair, even though it stinks, a true believer is not about to throw in the towel and lose. Others may or may not be able to spot the weaker link, and you probably won't get the earthly credit for your additional effort. But you want to know that you did everything you could to get to the finish line.

I often tell wives that I do *not* want to stand before God at the end of my life, and have Him say, "Why did you hinder your husband from doing everything I called him to do?" That would crush me! And I don't want Francis to have to coddle me and worry and not push so hard because I felt like I couldn't handle it. God is trustworthy. He can supply *all* our needs. And if you are focused on the mission, He will not only supply your needs but give you grace upon grace as you watch Him work and move and change lives right before your eyes. And then you will *really* cry, thinking, "I could have missed all of this because I wanted my daughter to stay at this school her whole life or because I was so afraid of how this might affect my son, or because I am just so selfish."

If we were honest with ourselves, we would admit that many times we don't want to have to put any effort into our walk with Christ. We don't want to put in the training time needed to keep our lives and our marriages focused on the mission. But how else is it going to happen?

> Rather train yourself for godliness; for while bodily training is of some value, godliness is of value in every way, as it holds promise for the present life and also for the life to come. The saying is trustworthy and deserving of full acceptance. (1 Timothy 4:7–9)

I love simple and straightforward passages like this. A godly life and marriage will not just happen. Spiritual muscles have to be continuously exercised, and your heart for the things of God has to be regularly stimulated. Not only did Paul give this command to train ourselves toward godliness, but immediately after he said: "to this end we toil and strive" (1 Timothy 4:10). It takes continual work. Paul had to remind the Philippians to "*work out* your own salvation with fear and trembling" (Phil. 2:12). Not to work *for* their salvation—that is a gift of God—but to work *out* their salvation. Then he reminded them of why they were working: "for it is God who works in you, both to will and to work for his good pleasure" (Phil. 2:13).

I can testify that the mission is far more appealing than the safety of the status quo. Yes, sometimes I am tempted to pursue an "ordinary" life. There are moments when I just want to be selfish and not think so hard about what God wants. But it's too late. Once you have experienced true life, there's no going back!

David urged us to "taste and see that the LORD is good" (Ps. 34:8), and that's what has happened for me. I have tasted what it's like to live a life that is more and more surrendered to Him. I have tasted and seen His love for others, and when He gives you that same love in your heart, it feels shallow and unfulfilling to go back to your old way of doing things. I have a taste in my mouth for steps of faith that draw you so near to Him you don't want to ever go back, even if He would let you.

These are desires that have come out of living missionally. I did not start with them. Honestly, I think my simple desire in the beginning was *not to miss God.* I clearly remember being on an airplane, looking out over the endless sky, and praying about what God wanted to do with our family. I was overwhelmed with the thought that we could get so caught up in our own lives, we could completely miss out on God's plans. It scared me a little. It scared me to surrender to God, but it scared me more to think of what I would miss if I didn't.

> Now this I say and testify in the Lord, that you must no longer walk as the Gentiles do, in the futility of their minds. They are darkened in their understanding, alienated from the life of God because of the ignorance that is in them, due to their hardness of heart. They have become callous and have given themselves up to sensuality, greedy to practice every kind of impurity. But that is not the way you learned Christ!—assuming that you have heard about him and were taught in him, as the truth is in Jesus, to put off your old self, which belongs to your former manner of life and is corrupt through deceitful desires, and to be renewed in the spirit of your minds, and to put on the new self, created after the likeness of God in true righteousness and holiness. (Ephesians 4:17–24)

Those who don't believe are going to live self-absorbed, greedy, sensual, indulgent lives.

But those who belong to Christ will be on a mission. They will put off that old, corrupted way of life and put on an entirely

new self! To be about the mission means we lay aside the things
that get in our way.

> Let us also lay aside every weight, and sin which
> clings so closely, and let us run with endurance
> the race that is set before us... (Hebrews 12:1)

Think again of the dedication of Olympic athletes. They
almost literally wear their underwear in front of millions of people
so that they will be as unhindered as possible. The slightest bulk in
clothing can slow them down, so they get rid of every unnecessary
obstacle.

What sin is hindering you right now? What is entangling you
and making it impossible for you to run the race well?

What about things that aren't necessarily sinful, but are still
distracting?

Fixing our eyes on Jesus means turning our eyes from whatever
else we are staring at. The television? YouTube? Shopping net-
works? Our own families? We will have to make conscious choices
throughout our lives in order to stay focused on the mission.

I remember one January day when Francis approached our
family with a challenge in regards to TV. He asked us to spend
equal amounts of time watching TV and reading the Bible for
a few months. So if we read for 30 minutes, we would be able
to watch TV for 30 minutes. I wish I could tell you we were all
instantly on board, but that was not the case. We had already
given up cable, so I thought we were doing pretty good just by

living off of Netflix. Plus, it's always a little uncomfortable to be asked to give up a "freedom." But who could argue? It made sense to train ourselves to give to God what He already deserved. (He deserves much more!)

It's training seasons like these that prepare us—including our kids—to stay focused on why we are here. God does give us a lot of freedom, but Peter reminds us what our freedom is for: "Live as people who are free, not using your freedom as a cover-up for evil, but living as servants of God" (1 Pet. 2:16).

I have had the privilege of watching other believers live as servants of God. I remember a woman who was so convicted about the amount of time she spent reading magazines that she cancelled her subscriptions in order to stay focused. I think of my friend Jan, who could not quote you a single line from a movie because she hasn't watched one in 15 years. But she can quote many, many Scriptures, which she uses to bless and encourage the women she disciples. I think of a young couple we know who could have purchased a home in a quiet, "safe" neighborhood, but chose instead to move into the inner city to love and disciple the people God surrounded them with. I think of a couple living in a two-bedroom apartment with their three kids, who opened up their home to a woman in need of a fresh start from addiction. And I think about a couple I met briefly, who had adopted several special needs orphans. They simply radiated honesty, love, and joy.

What an honor to witness God's people on a mission, to watch believers live out the gospel. It's compelling and attractive and reminds me why it's worth it to train ourselves for godliness.

If we are *not* making decisions in our lives that seem weird or radical to lukewarm people, we probably need to evaluate what's going on. Believers on a mission are going to look a little crazy to most of the world, just as the training regimen of an Olympic athlete looks a little crazy to us. What about your life indicates that you are not living for this world?

As a kid, our family went off-roading all the time. We would camp out in the desert for days—in the middle of nowhere—with no shower, a port-a-potty, and a Bunsen burner to cook all of our meals. At night, we would lay on a sand dune and feel like we could reach out and touch the stars. They took your breath away! I have such fond memories of these trips.

But after a few days, it was the smell of our own hair that took our breath away! With the sun beating down on us all day, and the dirt and grime from off-roading covering our skin, we were a sight to see. We would get interesting looks from people when we stopped for lunch on the way home. And when we returned home, there was never a more glorious feeling than taking a long hot shower, getting our clean comfy pajamas on, and falling into *our own beds.* Home! The most restful nights of sleep were those nights when we returned from a camping trip.

I can't help but make the connection to what's going on here in our lives. We are on a camping trip! It might be a 70 or 80 year camping trip, but that's all it is.

This world is not our home, and while we can function pretty well and enjoy ourselves to some degree, nothing will comfort us more than to get to our true home. To be truly cleansed from a lifelong battle with sin and the dirt of this world. To actually be clothed in righteousness, and, ultimately, to fall into the arms of Jesus.

It would have been laughable to see people rolling up into our campsite with their luxury vehicles, pre-built homes, pristine clothing, potted plants, and their personal gourmet chefs. That's not camping. When you're on a *temporary* camping trip, you are more than content with the basics. You don't need to set up a well decorated, cushy home, because you already know that the majority of your time will be spent pursuing the adventure. You have to round everybody up, get your gear, and *get on the road*.

I'm pretty sure that left to myself, without Francis' influence on my life, I would not have lived a very "missional" life. It's strange (and even scary) to imagine where my focus would be, had God not put me with my husband. He is one of the most eternally focused people I know, and I am so grateful for that. When we were dating, I admired his fear of the Lord, how serious he was about following Christ, and his high view of Scripture. It didn't hurt that he made me laugh all the time, and I always wanted to be around him.

After we married, I still admired these things, but now they were cramping my style! He thought through decisions in a way I never really had before, and at times I felt like a spiritual loser. It's funny to look back over 20 years later and realize how self-centered I was even about spiritual growth. Why doesn't this come naturally to me? Does this mean he thinks so little of me? Why do I have to give things up—it's not my conviction. Can't we just do things the way everyone else does?

But thank you, Lord. The more I grew in my faith, and the more my husband steadfastly led our home, the more freedom and joy and peace I experienced. To have someone by my side that will "count everything as loss because of the surpassing worth of knowing Christ Jesus my Lord" (Philip. 3:8) is my greatest earthly gift.

Sometimes things feel more "foreign" than they really are, because you just haven't done it enough. The beauty of deciding to live on purpose, with the mission in mind, is that it will become more and more familiar as you go along. The first few steps and changes feel awkward and difficult, but then this beautiful rhythm kicks in. You find that even though there are still moments of resistance (or temptation), you desire to stay on track. You don't want to miss out on the blessing that comes from fixing your eyes on what truly matters.

CONCLUSION: ENOUGH SAID

> "His master said to him, 'Well done, good and faithful servant. You have been faithful over a little; I will set you over much. Enter into the joy of your master.'" (Matthew 25:21)

Is there anything you want more than to hear "well done" come from God's lips?

Not "well said" or "well thought out," but "well *done*." Do something. Use your knowledge, gifts, and possessions today. You have a mission to pursue.

DO SOMETHING

The mission is always before us: make disciples. Your busy schedule, your unhealthy focus on your family, your pursuit of your own desires—these things don't negate the mission, they just show that you've been neglecting it. It's time to get yourselves focused on the mission again. In reality, this will involve every aspect of your life. Use the following suggestions to get yourself started, but don't stop here.

EVALUATE YOUR PURSUIT OF THE MISSION.

+ *Sit down with your spouse and honestly evaluate your devotion to the mission that God has given you.*

+ *What aspects of your life demonstrate that your God-given mission of making disciples means anything to you?*

+ *What aspects of your life stand in blatant disobedience to God's command to make disciples?*

+ *Thinking very practically, how can you begin to restructure your lives with the words "make disciples" at the center?*

TAKE IMMEDIATE ACTION.

+ *While this command requires a complete restructuring of your life, you also need to do something immediately. You can't keep putting God's mission off.*

✦ *With your spouse (and perhaps your whole family),
decide on at least one thing you can do to refocus
yourselves on God's mission. Consider things like:*

> *Finding a way to serve someone else. If your church
> has ministry opportunities, dive in immediately.
> If you know someone who needs a meal or some
> money, help them out right away. If you know
> someone who could use some encouragement, gather
> your family and make it happen in a creative way.*

> *Removing (at least temporarily) some of those
> things that may be good, but are functioning as
> distractions: like TV, shopping, hobbies, etc.*

> *Talking to your pastor about what your church is
> doing to fulfill God's mission and how you can help
> (if you're not currently part of a church, this is the
> place to start).*

> *Initiating a conversation with someone that you
> can begin discipling or being discipled by. This may
> sound like a huge step, but it's important. If you
> don't know where to start, we've put together a lot
> of material to help at multiplymovement.com.*

5

Is there Hope for Us?

MARRIAGE IN LIGHT OF GOD'S PROMISES

"I told you! I told you it would be worth it!!! This is unbelievable!!!!!!!"

I imagine shouting that one day when I see Lisa and the kids in heaven. They will no longer be my wife and kids, but we will love each other more than ever. I picture myself looking them in the eyes and saying, "I told you He would come through! I knew He would be true to His promises. I knew that every sacrifice would be worth it. This is insane! He is amazing!!!"

That is the perfect ending for me. That's what I consider "happily ever after." So now I work backwards—what can I do today to ensure that my story ends that way? We should all make decisions based on hindsight. Picture yourself standing before God at the moment of your death, looking back at your time on earth. At that moment, what will you regret? What will you cherish? Now, what would your life be like if you made your decisions on that basis?

We can be sure that we are heaven-bound if we trust in Jesus. But God blesses us even further—He promises to reward any sacrifices made lovingly for His kingdom (Mark 10:28–30). In fact, it is impossible to please God unless we believe in His rewards.

> Without faith it is impossible to please him, for whoever would draw near to God must believe that he exists and that he rewards those who seek him. (Hebrews 11:6)

I used to think that it was wrong to earn rewards by serving God. After all, shouldn't we just want to serve Him because of all that He has done for us? Hasn't He already given us far more than we deserve? Yes. Definitely. But we can't get around the fact that Jesus actually tells us to "store up treasures in heaven" (Matt. 6:20). All throughout the New Testament, we are told about what we gain by serving Him.

You should do a study on "rewards" sometime. The New Testament refers to rewards more often than you might think. If you want to begin your study right now, start by looking up the following passages: 1 Cor. 3:10–15; 2 Cor. 4:17–18; Mark 9:38–50, 10:28–30; Matt. 5:1–12, 6:1-8, 6:16–21, 10:40-42; Luke 6:20–36; Col. 3:23–25; and Rev. 11:16–18.

These blessings actually keep us from becoming self-righteous. It takes the attention off *our* sacrifice, and places it on *His* generosity. Eternity will not be about "look at what *I* sacrificed" but rather "look at what *He* gave me!" God will be the center of attention. We will spend eternity marveling at the "immeasurable riches of His grace" (Eph. 2:7).

God guarantees these rewards, and He loves it when we pursue them. So we should go through life joyfully resisting temptations, sharing the gospel, and sacrificing for the poor, knowing that future rewards far outweigh any suffering.

ETERNITY CHANGES EVERYTHING

"If in Christ we have hope in this life only, we are of all people most to be pitied" (1 Cor. 15:19). It's true. Paul is to be pitied if there is no resurrection of the dead. The reverse is also true: Paul is to be envied if there is a resurrection. If you could see him now, you would be jealous. You would want to switch places, wouldn't you? All of the sacrifice in Paul's life earned him a reward that he has been enjoying for the past two thousand years. He hasn't an ounce of regret for the sacrifices he made on earth.

> So we do not lose heart. Though our outer self is wasting away, our inner self is being renewed day by day. For this light momentary affliction is preparing for us *an eternal weight of glory beyond all comparison*, as we look not to the things that are seen but to the things that are unseen. For the things that are seen are transient, but the things that are unseen are eternal. (2 Corinthians 4:16–18, emphasis added)

Stare at the unseen. The eternal. Don't become blinded by the transient.

We spend far too much time looking at temporary things. That is exactly what Satan wants you to do: ignore reality. Ignore eternity. Doubt the things that God says are true and significant. The devil bombards you with temporary issues. He is trying to make you love things that don't last. How is he doing?

Try something: Close your eyes and forget about everything that is temporary. Then talk to God only about those things that are unseen and eternal. It takes a lot of effort and deep thinking, but I prayed that you would do this. So please take a few moments and try it.

ANTICIPATE

I don't have any statistics to prove this, but based on my experience, I'd bet that at least 95% of American "Christians" would choose not to leave their families today if they were given the choice to be with Jesus. You can justify that all you want, but something is off. Paul recognized the value of staying on earth to minister to the people around him, but his burning desire was to be with Jesus (Philip. 1:21–26). If you'd rather watch your kids grow up than see the face of your Savior today, you don't grasp the beauty of God. If you worry about what would happen to your children if you were gone, you don't understand the providence of God. Pray for a deeper understanding of His worth and sovereignty. Pray earnestly until you are infatuated with seeing His face.

When Lisa and I were engaged, I jokingly said that I wanted Christ to return, but I was hoping He would wait until after my honeymoon. While I was no angel, I was by the grace of God able to maintain my virginity until marriage. So the marriage night was something I was willing to put off heaven for. I said it jokingly, but God knows I meant it. I valued Him, but not that much. I wanted Him, but not most.

There's always something. Marriage, the birth of a child, watching the kids grow up, watching your grandkids grow up. There's always something immediate and attractive that keeps us from anticipating heaven. For some, your lack of excitement could be caused by a lack of meditation. You don't dwell on heaven much. But for others, the lack of anticipation could stem from something deeper: a lack of faith.

FIGHT DOUBT

Recently I was asked to preach on God's faithfulness. I had preached on many of God's attributes over the years, but never specifically on His faithfulness. The more I studied and prayed, the more it was apparent that I had trust issues. Like everyone reading this book, I have been lied to throughout my entire life. And I have lied to others. Even if I say that I trust someone, it means I trust them maybe 85 percent. The days of 100 percent trust disappeared sometime during childhood. While I trust my wife more than anyone, it's still only in the 90 percent range. Ok, maybe upper nineties.

As life goes on, my skepticism has only grown. I used to get shocked by people's lies. Now I'm surprised by honesty. Some of you may not struggle with this, but most of us do. And I don't think it is necessarily wrong to have this kind of skepticism. Jesus was skeptical.

> Now when he was in Jerusalem at the Passover Feast,
> many believed in his name when they saw the signs

that he was doing. But Jesus on his part did not entrust himself to them, because he knew all people and needed no one to bear witness about man, for he himself knew what was in man. (John 2:23–25)

We are all liars to some degree. So it shouldn't surprise us that we are skeptics. We know that we have lied, so it's safe to assume that others do too. This is why we need contracts. A person's word is not enough. That is just the world we live in. But this becomes sinful when our habit of distrust spills over onto God's promises. Before we know it, we are treating His Word like everyone else's words.

Do you catch yourself being guarded? You go into situations expecting the worst so you can't be disappointed. People have let you down, and you refuse to be hurt again. You protect yourself from disappointment, but in the process you have lost your ability to hope. God doesn't want His children to live this way. He wants us beaming with anticipation. He wants us confident and thrilled about our future in heaven. He wants us "boasting in our hope" (Heb. 3:6). Don't allow the lies of the past to kill your joy over God's promises for the future. Celebrate heaven today. Though people will lie to us, God never will.

> Paul, a servant of God and an apostle of Jesus Christ, for the sake of the faith of God's elect and their knowledge of the truth, which accords with godliness, *in hope of eternal life, which God, who never lies, promised before the ages began* and at the proper

time manifested in his word through the preaching
with which I have been entrusted by the command
of God our Savior... (Titus 1:1–3, emphasis added)

Test yourself right now. On a scale of one to ten, how excited
are you about heaven today? How much did the promise of heaven
affect your attitude and actions last week?

It made me sad when I realized that I doubted God's promises.
I prayed that God would help me trust to the point of anticipation.
Do you remember those times as a kid when you could hardly
sleep on Christmas Eve because you were so excited about opening
presents in the morning? That anticipation showed that you had
no doubt. We should have an even greater anticipation of Jesus. If
you are not "eagerly waiting for Him" (Heb. 9:28), something is
off. Ask God to restore hope in your life. Not the kind of "hope"
where you vaguely wish something would happen, but the kind of
hope that anchors your soul (Heb. 6:19). Meditate on His promises
and pray for faith.

Know therefore that the LORD your God is God, the
faithful God who keeps covenant and steadfast love
with those who love him and keep his command-
ments, to a thousand generations... (Deuteronomy
7:9)

If we are faithless, he remains faithful—for he cannot deny himself. (2 Timothy 2:13)

It is His very nature to be faithful. There are a couple of things that God cannot do: He cannot stop being faithful; He cannot lie. So *rest* and *rejoice* in His promises.

IMAGINE

It's hard to imagine what the future will be like, but we should. The Bible describes our future existence for that very reason. God wants us to be excited about it. Our excitement proves that we believe in His resurrection and our own.

I thought about trying to describe the joys of heaven to you. I want you to feel it, to be thrilled about where we are headed. But my words can't do it justice. Instead, it would be better if you read this excerpt from the last pages of the Bible. Revelation uses enough vivid imagery in describing heaven to make our imagination run wild with anticipation. This is our destiny. Heaven and earth come together and God Himself lives with us. Read this passage slowly, trying to picture it in your mind's eye. And keep reading it over and over until you find yourself longing for heaven with a tangible excitement.

> Then I saw a new heaven and a new earth, for the first heaven and the first earth had passed away, and the sea was no more. And I saw the holy city, new Jerusalem, coming down out of heaven from God, prepared as a bride adorned for her husband. And I heard a loud voice from the throne saying, "Behold, the dwelling place of God is with man. He will dwell with them, and they will be his

people, and God himself will be with them as their God. He will wipe away every tear from their eyes, and death shall be no more, neither shall there be mourning, nor crying, nor pain anymore, for the former things have passed away."

And he who was seated on the throne said, "Behold, I am making all things new." Also he said, "Write this down, for these words are trustworthy and true." And he said to me, "It is done! I am the Alpha and the Omega, the beginning and the end. To the thirsty I will give from the spring of the water of life without payment. The one who conquers will have this heritage, and I will be his God and he will be my son. But as for the cowardly, the faithless, the detestable, as for murderers, the sexually immoral, sorcerers, idolaters, and all liars, their portion will be in the lake that burns with fire and sulfur, which is the second death."

And I saw no temple in the city, for its temple is the Lord God the Almighty and the Lamb. And the city has no need of sun or moon to shine on it, for the glory of God gives it light, and its lamp is the Lamb. By its light will the nations walk, and the kings of the earth will bring their glory into it, and its gates will never be shut by day—and there will be no night there. They will bring into it the glory and the honor of the nations. But nothing unclean will ever enter it, nor anyone who does what is detestable or false, but only those who are written in the Lamb's book of life. (Revelation 21:1–8, 22–27)

DON'T GIVE UP. IT WILL ALL BE WORTH IT —Lisa

Having a marriage characterized by humility, and focused on the mission, will require commitment and sacrifice. But it's not all work and no play. God's promises include benefits that affect our time here on earth, as well as in heaven.

Do not be deceived: God is not mocked, for whatever one sows, that will he also reap. For the one who sows to his own flesh will from the flesh reap corruption, but the one who sows to the Spirit will from the Spirit reap eternal life. (Galatians 6:7-8)

If that is the case, we can be confident that as we sow to the Spirit in our marriages, we will reap spiritual blessings in our marriages. Have you ever stopped to consider that? It says the fruit of the Spirit is love, joy, peace, patience, kindness, goodness, faithfulness, gentleness, and self-control (Gal. 5:22–23). I don't know many people who would look at that list and not want all of it. These are things that you *will* experience as you live a Spirit-filled life.

So how do we "sow to the Spirit" in our marriages? I realized as I read over that Scripture that it's a pretty heady concept. If we want to get excited about reaping the spiritual benefits, we need to know that we can sow the right stuff.

Practically speaking, we have to start with the seed of prayer. When is the last time you prayed specifically and earnestly for your marriage? How about specifically and earnestly for your husband or wife? Do you realize that very few people are going to be praying faithfully for your marriage and your spouse? I don't want to sound dramatic, but prayer changes everything! Prayer opens up that line of communication with the Holy Spirit. There is no other way to invite the sensitivity you need to even hear the voice of the Lord. Yes, we must read and know Scripture, but without talking to God in prayer, we are crippled. Jesus went away from the crowds many times to speak to His Father alone. Who are we to think we can function without it?

I want you to consider the lives of the most godly people you know. Think of what sets them apart. I'm willing to guess that they are characterized by that list in Galatians. Loving, joyful, peaceful, kind. Am I right? Ask them how they came to enjoy such spiritual blessings. Without exception, every godly person I know is a man or woman of prayer, the Word, and action.

One of the most amazing promises from God is that He will hear and answer us as we humbly cry out to Him.

> In my distress I called upon the Lord;
>   to my God I cried for help.
> From his temple he heard my voice,
>   and my cry to him reached his ears. (Psalm 18:6)

The promise is not that we will always get the answer we desire, but that God will hear. He will listen to your cry, and if your desire is to live for Him, He will lead you in the right way.

In the midst of Paul's farming illustration (sowing to the Spirit), he gives one of my favorite promises. Farmers have to be so patient. They prepare the ground, they work the soil, they plant the seed, they water and care for the crop, they protect it from outside influences, and, finally, they harvest their crop and enjoy the fruits of their labor.

> Let us not become weary in doing good, for at the proper time we will reap a harvest if we do not give up. (Galatians 6:9, NIV)

I know that some of you are tired. I know that many of you struggle every day to keep your mind and heart focused on the right things, especially in a difficult marriage. I bet some days you just want to give up. This promise is what you hold on to. You will reap a harvest if you don't give up.

> For this light momentary affliction is preparing for us an eternal weight of glory beyond all comparison. (2 Corinthians 4:17)

There is an eternal weight of glory that you do not want to give up! Eternal. Glory. That is a promise worth holding on to! Don't get so caught up in what your marriage is or is not that you forget what your life is going to look like for all of eternity, the promises you will enjoy for thousands of years! You cannot underestimate how powerful an example it is when a believer acts on God's promises, even when they won't be fulfilled until we get to heaven.

Every now and then I come to the same realization: it is very easy to desire things from marriage that we are able to get from God, and should get from God. He is the ultimate keeper of promises.

Sometimes I expect to receive certain feelings of worth from my husband. I want to be lifted up and adored and made to feel wanted. These aren't necessarily bad things, but now and then the Lord gently reminds me, *"I am the One who gives you worth. I am the One who perfectly meets your needs. Come to Me to be lifted up, and sometimes, even, brought low. Because then you won't place unnecessary burdens on your husband."*

When something feels "off" between Francis and me, I have learned to examine my walk with God *first*. Far too many wives are looking to their husbands to meet needs they simply cannot meet, and vice versa. Far too many marriages are riddled with unrealistic—ungodly—expectations. God promises to meet all of your needs (Philip. 4:19), He promises never to leave you (Heb. 13:5), He promises that nothing can separate you from His love (Rom. 8:38–39) and that no one can snatch you out of His hand (John 10:27–29). If we want our marriages to be healthy, we have to first believe God's promises and look to Him before we look to our spouses.

I clearly remember the first time this hit me like a ton of bricks. Francis and I had gone away for an anniversary trip, and over dinner I asked him to tell me one thing I could do to be a better wife (something we ask each other periodically). He told me he felt like I relied too much on him, and had too many expectations. He wanted me to rely more on God, and go to Him first.

This caught me so off guard. Honestly, I thought I was cruising along just fine, and it shook me up a bit. I searched my heart, wanting to defend myself, but God showed me very clearly that my husband was right. It struck me that in my efforts to be a submissive wife who followed her husband's lead, I had become lazy in my own walk with God. I bypassed essential time spent at the feet of Jesus and went straight to my husband with everything. Not only was this exhausting for him, it was crippling my relationship with God.

So much of what we need in our spiritual lives is gained through "wrestling" with God in prayer and through "waiting upon the Lord" and learning to recognize His voice. I often tell wives that we need to bring our prayers and struggles and desires to the Lord *first*. God may well use our husbands to meet many of our needs, but God is the ultimate source of everything we need. It's not that we hide our needs and struggles from our husbands, it's simply a matter of where to start. Our husbands will be huge failures if we expect them to be God. But if we expect God to be God, then our husbands can excel at being husbands.

It could be that much of the heartache surrounding your marriage is a lack of spiritual connection between you and Christ.

It could be that you are so relationally "needy" because you have neglected your spiritual needs. It's time to strengthen your walk with God!

As a woman, I hear a lot of talk these days about being a "strong" woman. What does that mean? What does a strong woman look like?

When my husband and I were in Ethiopia recently, I was struck by the life of the women there. Quite frankly, it was overwhelming to think about what it would feel like to work as hard as they did—physically hard—without seeing very much progress. What would it be like to live without running water in my home? Who would walk the mile or two every day to fill up our plastic jug with enough water to meet our basic needs? What would I cook in the small fire burning *inside* my very small hut? Would it cross my mind that I had worn the exact same dirty top and skirt for days on end? When my children were cold in the night, how could I help them without the ability to flip on a heater and simply fall back asleep?

But these women live this reality every single day. And they were able to smile at me. They are strong. I'll never forget making eye contact with some of these women as they sat with their little ones, waiting to see if they would make it into the feeding program. I felt like we communicated with no words, "We are both mothers, we both want to care for our children." I would try to say with my eyes, "You are *loved*—by me, yes, but more importantly, by God."

One day as we were driving back from one of these villages, I saw the most amazing tree perched on a hill. It had a thick and sturdy trunk, with gorgeous full branches of a beautiful shade of green. I felt the Lord say, "That is what a strong woman looks like." A strong woman has waited patiently while her roots grew down deep into the Word of God. Over time, she becomes unshakeable in her faith. She starts bearing fruit naturally and is full of life. People are attracted to her strength and growth, and many find rest and peace as they lean on her. And when storms and trials come, as they always do, they will not be able to take her down. A few branches may be lost or pruned away, but in their place comes new growth, new life.

This is what I long to be! A strong woman who is anchored in God's promises.

But it starts by setting down your roots in God's Word. It will not happen as you stand up for yourself, and demand attention, and fight for yourself. It will happen as you stand *in Christ*, and demand that *He* gets *your attention*, and fight for *His* glory.

The beautiful thing is that as we pursue this, God takes His rightful place in our lives. It says in Scripture, "The joy of the Lord is your *strength*" (Neh. 8:10). Joy is also listed as a fruit of the Spirit in Galatians. You will never find true, lasting joy in some*one* or some*thing*. Marriage is not the source of joy, though many of us assume that it is. Joy is something we bring into our marriages because we are being filled with joy in our walk with God, and because we are confident of His promises.

It's time to stop looking to your marriage and your spouse to do the things that God promises to do for us. True strength, true joy, true fulfillment—these are all promised to us by God, and they can only come from Him.

CONCLUSION: FOCUS

Peter says that a person can become "so nearsighted that he is blind" (2 Peter 1:8). We are capable of getting so focused on temporary things that we become blind to the things that actually matter. It's crazy how a flat tire can cause you to forget about your future inheritance, eternal security, and the grace that God is going to pour out on you for all eternity. We quickly lose the joy of our salvation and future glory because of something so temporary. We become focused on the here and now. It's not that we shouldn't pay attention to obvious problems before us, but we need to look at them with an eternal lens. And we can't let anything rob us of our joy.

At any moment, you are going to be taken into a new existence. You will not care at all about some of the things you currently obsess with. We should have the attitude of the shrewd manager mentioned in Luke 16. He knew his time was limited in his current position, so he wisely set himself up for the future. My prayer is that God's promises about the future would shape our marriages in the present.

DO SOMETHING

It may seem impractical to talk about God's promises of the future and then say, "Do something now!" But that's really how it's supposed to work. God tells us about the future so we will know how to conduct ourselves now (cf., 2 Pet. 3:11). Use the following suggestions to guide your thinking, but don't stop here. For the duration of your married life, you should be thinking about God's promises regarding the future and adjusting your relationship with your spouse accordingly.

MEDITATE ON HEAVEN.

+ *Spend some time actually dwelling on the reality of heaven. To guide your thinking, I encourage you to read through Revelation 21–22. But read slowly. Take in the pictures. Picture yourself in John's shoes as he watched this vision of the end unfolding.*

+ *Now imagine what it will be like. How will it feel? What problems will this reality resolve? Why do we long for this so deeply? As vividly as you can, experience what it will be like to live in a place that has no sun or moon because it is illuminated by the very face of God. Let this kind of meditation heal your soul and fuel your hope.*

+ *Finally, consider how this vision of the end should shape your present in general, and your marriage in particular. Write down a few thoughts of how your marriage can and should be shaped by God's promises of how the world will end. Compare these thoughts with your spouse and have an honest discussion of how this vision can truly become central in your marriage.*

EVALUATE YOUR HOPE.

+ *Hope is a biblical concept, but even as Christians our hope is often misplaced. Evaluate where your hope truly lies. Be brutally honest.*

1. *In what ways do you place your hope in your spouse?*

2. *Who do you look to for fulfillment, for joy, for the meeting of your needs, etc.?*

3. *In what areas are you doing well in terms of placing your hope in God alone?*

4. *In what areas are you doing poorly in this regard?*

✦ *After you've honestly assessed yourself in this regard, talk with your spouse about your conclusions. See if he or she agrees or has other points to add or subtract. This is a vulnerable and sensitive activity, so be sure to be gentle, loving, and honest. Any honest explanations of each other's weaknesses are offered for the sake of growing more like Christ.*

✦ *Discuss practical ways that you can focus your hope more on Christ, and ways that you can help each other do this better.*

✦ *Commit to praying for each other regarding the things you've discussed here.*

What's Really Best for the Kids?

PARENTING TO THE GLORY OF GOD

"Five kids?"

"You poor guy!"

"There are ways to prevent that, you know!"

I hear statements like these all the time. I hear them from unbelievers and believers alike. The popular belief is that a child or two might be a blessing, but there must be something wrong with you if you have more. It's such a bizarre way of thinking to me because I am so crazy about my kids. Maybe it sounds cheesy, but I can honestly say that one of my biggest struggles is making sure I don't love my kids too much! If I'm not careful, they can become the chief recipients of my love and affections rather than Christ. Some people struggle with neglecting their kids, seeing them as burdens. Others, like me, struggle by overemphasizing their relationship with their children.

The truth is that God created family, and He wants us to find pleasure in our families for His glory. There is a way to love our children while leading them into a lifestyle of worship and mission. And this will ultimately bring the most fulfillment to us and to our children. Now and for all eternity.

Here is God's opinion of children:

> Behold, children are a heritage from the LORD,
>   the fruit of the womb a reward.
> Like arrows in the hand of a warrior
>   are the children of one's youth.
> Blessed is the man
>   who fills his quiver with them!
> He shall not be put to shame
>   when he speaks with his enemies in the gate.
>   (Psalm 127:3–5)

Like a quarterback praising the rest of his team for enabling his success, children were meant to be the cause of a person's praise. God says a man will "not be put to shame" *because* of his many children who stand behind him. Why now are children so often regarded as "in the way," hindrances to the things we really want to do?

Since the beginning of time, people have envied large families. They would look at them and think, "You're so lucky." Over the past 20 years in America, the attitude switched to, "I would hate to be in your shoes."

While there are a variety of reasons for this new attitude (such as the financial expense, the added responsibility, or the loss of freedom), I believe poor parenting may be the main cause of this negative view toward children. A pack of disrespectful kids is like a quiver full of crooked arrows that might actually come flying back at you!

RAISE BLESSINGS, NOT BURDENS

What is a great parent? Is it someone who does everything for his or her child? Or is it someone who trains the child to do things? If a kid can't tie his shoe, the parent has failed. Right? If he can't cut his own steak, can we really call the parenting successful? But why do we stop there? Shouldn't we expect our grown sons and daughters to do their own laundry, clean the house, and eventually work a job and make money?

What is it that motivates parents to consistently do everything for their children? Is it a desire to be needed? A desire to be liked, thanked, and praised? A need to be "friends" with their children? Or maybe it's just easier sometimes to do it ourselves. But the truth is, we are doing a disservice to our children by constantly serving them and enabling them to be lazy. This is how kids end up being burdens. This is why people don't see children as blessings. This is why they are not like "arrows in the quiver." We don't sharpen them and never use them. They're just sticks we carry around. They have no purpose, we never put them to any use—we just keep carrying them around.

But it's amazing how much our children can accomplish when they need to, when they have a mission, a responsibility.

This is similar to what we do in the church. Leaders cater to people rather than teaching them to be caterers. This makes them over-dependent. So when they're left on their own, they fail. They are burdens to us because we don't expect them to carry their weight and help carry the weight of others. Pastors of big churches have big burdens. Instead of being blessings, the people become burdens. But that's for another book.

My kids are some of my best friends. I think that's a good thing. But we must be careful that we don't work so hard towards our friendships that we forget we are the parents. They don't need just another friend. They need an authority figure, an example, something their buddies can't offer them. God has placed you in your child's life in such a way that you represent His loving authority. He has given you the responsibility of raising your children, teaching them how to serve, preparing them for the future.

PARENTING IN LIGHT OF GOD'S GLORY

Lisa and I want to raise children who love Jesus far more than they love us. We want them to trust Him more than us, to enjoy Him more than us, to find more security in Him than in us. And we are convinced that the best way to teach this is to demonstrate it. We have to make it clear to our children that we love God more than we love them.

Children are more perceptive than many parents think. They can tell if our words are only words. We can say all day long that we love Jesus more than them, but they see where our time and resources go. They aren't blind to our affections nor to our lack of prayer and worship. Kids know when we fake it.

Maybe you'll spend years thinking you've fooled your kids. But it's only a matter of time before they are old enough to reflect.

After all, don't you know the truth about your parents? When you became a young adult, weren't you able to look back at the relationship of your parents and know the truth? You knew whether their love for each other was actually deep or just a show. You know now whether their faith was a religious duty or a source of life. You know whether they loved you more than they loved Jesus.

I speak with many young adults. A new thing is happening in the Christian church in America. Young people who see the worth of Jesus are fighting resentment towards parents who lived lukewarm lives. Parents who idolized their kids and expected praise in return are receiving the opposite. These young adults are falling in love with Jesus despite the example of their parents, and some even try to respectfully rebuke their parents. What's most beautiful is that some parents have actually repented after seeing the example of their children!

While there are some inspiring success stories, this is definitely not the norm. Statistics show that the vast majority of kids who grow up in these nice, comfortable, church-going homes where family is idolized walk away from the church once they turn eighteen, never to return. In many of these cases, the kids love their parents, but don't love Jesus.

Here's a question every parent should be asking: What will break my heart more? If my kids don't end up loving me? Or if they don't end up loving Jesus? Seriously contemplate that question.

What's nice is that if your kids truly love Jesus, they will truly love you. It's guaranteed. I have yet to find a person who loves Jesus who is not deeply grateful for parents who "truly lived it out." Not only that, but those who love Jesus obey his commands

(John 14:15), and Jesus commands us to love the people around us deeply (Mark 12:28–31, 1 John 4:19–21).

In addition to being a godly example, God asks us to be the ones who teach our children about Him. Sadly, most parents neglect this responsibility and assume their Sunday school teachers and youth group leaders have this covered. While it's wonderful to have additional support, it doesn't change the fact that God commands parents to teach their children to love God and His commands (Deut. 6:4–8).

There are practical things that Lisa and I do to teach our children about the glory of God. We consistently use Scripture to remind them of God's holiness. We can't just tell our kids to believe in God, we need to explain to them what He is like. Try this with your kids. Describe the glory of God. Take a passage like 1 Timothy 6:15-16 and break it down for them:

> "...[our Lord Jesus Christ] who is the blessed and only Sovereign, the King of kings and Lord of lords, who alone has immortality, who dwells in unapproachable light, whom no one has ever seen or can see. To him be honor and eternal dominion. Amen."

Explain to them that God is the *"only Sovereign"*—that He is the only One who has control. They need to know from an early age that mom and dad can't control life, and neither can they. All things are in His hands.

Make sure they understand what it means to be *"the King of kings."* All authority belongs to Him. So they need to respect Him more than they respect mom and dad. Show them that mom and dad submit to Jesus above all others, that when Jesus calls you to do something, you do it immediately and without question. Explain that to your kids. And show them what it looks like.

Let them know that every breath they take is a gift from God because He "*alone has immortality.*" Every plant, animal, and person borrows life from Him. So we live each day making the most of the life He gave us.

The sooner they begin to comprehend the glory of God, the better. They need to know that He "*dwells in unapproachable light.*" He is not like us. We can't even look upon Him. They must know that there is a massive gap between God and them.

Because of His sovereignty, authority, power, and holiness, we live our lives for His glory and not our own. We center our lives around His "*honor and eternal dominion.*" Our kids must be taught and shown that the world does not revolve around them—it revolves around Jesus. We live for Him.

Almost every child goes through the "egocentric" stage where she believes that the world revolves around her. When she cries, she observes adults scurrying to get a bottle or blanket or racing to rock her in their arms. She is the center of attention whenever she enters a room.

That is pretty natural for infants. And small children do indeed need extra attention. The problem is when this is still the norm at four or five or ten or sixteen or thirty. Sadly, many people find themselves at the end of their lives, still believing the world revolves (or should revolve) around them. Good parenting can curb that mindset at an early age.

Make sure that prayer does not become casual. Even at meal-times. When it's time to pray, Lisa and I are strict about turning off electronics, and we don't let the kids run around. We use these times to remind the family that we worship a holy God who deserves our respect. He is the center of attention, and we cater to His majesty. We are not just going through a ritual or continuing a tradition. We are thanking a God who dwells in unapproachable light. Prayer is sacred in our house because God is sacred. No one is allowed to disrespect God in our house. Our kids know that they are not to disturb mom or dad when they are talking to God because He is more important than they are.

While we try to speak about God throughout the day, we have found that bedtime is probably the best time for conversation. Our kids always prefer to talk rather than go to bed, so we take advantage of it. We listen to their stories about the day and we use every opportunity to remind them that God should be central in all that they do. We share about times during the day when we didn't "feel like" obeying God, but we did anyways. We always want to help them to see that we also struggle with selfishness, and that it's a fight for all of us to live for His glory instead of our own.

We take opportunities to teach our kids the importance of honoring their teachers and every authority figure because God placed them there (Rom. 13). This is critical because their lack of respect for authority is a form of arrogance that quickly spills over into a lack of respect for God.

> Children, obey your parents in the Lord, for this
> is right. "Honor your father and mother" (this is

> the first commandment with a promise), "that it
> may go well with you and that you may live long
> in the land." Fathers, do not provoke your chil-
> dren to anger, but bring them up in the discipline
> and instruction of the Lord. (Ephesians 6:1–4)

According to this passage, there are deep theological reasons to teach your kids to be respectful of authority. Children who disrespect their parents are disrespecting God. They are neglecting His commands and entering a pattern a rebellion.

I have never allowed any of my children to speak disrespect-fully to Lisa or myself. We exercise authority so they have a picture of authority. It's not about a power trip. As a dad, my job is to paint a picture of God by the way I act. Since we do not worship a weak God who permits disrespect, I refuse to be a weak dad who allows his kids to talk back. Children who grow up ruling the house will soon find themselves questioning God's right to give commands that go against how they think or feel. Those who grow up in a home where loving leadership is exemplified are not guaranteed to respect God, but at least they know how it would look.

PARENTING IN LIGHT OF THE GOSPEL

The truth of the gospel has huge implications for parenting. As believers, we know that our righteousness comes from God and our ability to live godly lives comes from the Holy Spirit. As parents, sometimes we forget that this will be true of our children as well. God is our only hope. God is their only hope. If the Spirit is not in them, then all of our parenting will amount to nothing more than behavior modification. Without the Spirit, our children are bound to rebel. But the Spirit of God changes everything. If He is working within our children, then we can trust Him to be working when and how He sees fit.

Years ago, our oldest daughter was struggling deeply. It was obvious to me that her faith consisted of little more than reciting Christian statements she had heard throughout her life. I did not see any fruit of the Spirit, and sin was the rule in her life. It's not that she didn't do some good things, but there's a big difference between performing some good deeds and the supernatural work of the Spirit.

Honestly, it was a sad time with many tears. At one point, Lisa asked me, "Do you think we failed as parents?" I responded by saying that I didn't think so. We had shown her an example of two people who love Jesus, family, and others. She had seen the Holy Spirit working in us and through us. I know our marriage and parenting have never been perfect, but I believed we had displayed for her a God-centered marriage and family.

The salvation of my children is my most heart-felt prayer request. During this time, we realized there was nothing we could do for our daughter. So we prayed. A lot. Only God could open her eyes, give her faith, and cause her to love Him. We knew we could give her more restrictions, but that would only modify her behavior temporarily. It wouldn't change her heart. God made it clear that the Holy Spirit was our only hope. Without Him, the best we could do was find ways to keep her from pursuing what her heart desired. Yet from everything I read in Scripture, if the Holy Spirit entered her, she would become a new person. There would be a change of nature where sin would no longer be her master, but righteousness would.

Then it happened. I'll never forget the day she told me that the Holy Spirit entered her. We were excited, but a bit skeptical. We saw immediate changes in her life but wondered if it would last. After a few weeks, then months, it was obvious that everything really did change. Years later, I still thank God for His grace in her life. She is a new creation. She's not perfect, but she's getting there. Now, rather than wanting to lock her in a room to keep her from carrying out her sin, we confidently release her to be a light to the world. This is what the Holy Spirit does.

Seeing the Holy Spirit in the lives of our children has led Lisa and I to let go. As we see the Spirit working, we slowly release our leadership and teach them to follow the leadership of the Holy Spirit. As John the Baptist said of Jesus, "He must increase, I must decrease" (John 3:30). That should be our attitude in parenting. The goal is to transition our children from total dependence on us to total dependence on Him. Our job is to teach them how to follow their true Father, their true Master. Then we let go because we have returned them to their rightful Owner. Entrusting our children to God's care shows our trust in God; continually clinging to our control over them shows the opposite.

This doesn't mean that we don't continue to play a significant role in their lives. It just means that we understand that our role is to constantly lead them back to God, back to the truth of the gospel. We must constantly remind our children of the power they possess in Christ, just as Paul did with Timothy (2 Tim. 1:6–7). As believers, we should always "consider how to stir up one another to love and good works" (Heb 10:24). This is a lifelong responsibility toward all believers, including our children. To put it simply, we always want to be a blessing, not a necessity. God is the only thing our children truly *need*, but we pray that He will make us a blessing to our children throughout their lives.

As I write this, I recognize that many people have children who aren't following Jesus. Perhaps that's you. You haven't seen the fruit of the Spirit in your kids and it breaks your heart. You don't know where to begin because your children have rejected the gospel. Or maybe they would never verbally deny Jesus, but they do so by their actions. First, let me say that I am sorry. Lisa and I can think of no deeper pain. In all honesty, I have yet to find valid words of comfort for Christian parents with unbelieving kids. As Paul described, many of us live with "great sorrow and unceasing anguish" (Rom. 9:2) because people we love dearly are rejecting Christ. In an odd way, there is comfort in realizing that the same Paul who rejoiced in all circumstances and told us to rejoice in the Lord always (Phil. 4:4) experienced this kind of deep-seated anguish.

The only encouragement I can think of is to remind you of the power of prayer. I have heard so many stories of miraculously answered prayers, and I have experienced this many times myself. Continue to fast and pray for your children. Continue to saturate yourself and your children in Scripture, knowing that there is power in God's Word. Continue to live in such a way that your kids cannot deny the presence of God in your life, even if they don't want Him for themselves.

As Christian parents, we have responsibilities in light of the gospel regardless of how our children respond. As God rules the earth, we must lead our homes. As God is free to punish and reward, we must prayerfully punish and reward our children in a way that glorifies God. As God forgives, we must demonstrate His forgiveness when our kids sin. As God has shown unconditional love, we must sacrifice for our children regardless of their actions. They must see the gospel brought to life when they observe our parenting. We strive to demonstrate a beautiful picture of Christ in hopes that they will find Him attractive and give their lives to knowing Him.

PARENTING IN LIGHT OF CHRIST'S EXAMPLE

Years ago, one of my daughters came home from school and showed me a test she had failed. I saw the disappointment in her eyes, but also the fear of how I was going to react. She and I both knew that the F was the result of laziness, not incompetence. So we both knew that consequences were in order. But that night, I decided to use the opportunity to teach her about grace. Instead of disciplining her, I took her out to dinner, a movie, and ice cream. I explained that I was doing this to illustrate what God has done for us through Christ. Despite our sin, He withholds His wrath and showers us with blessings.

We had a great evening, but the best part was the next day. When her friends said goodbye to her the previous day, they knew she was on her way to tell me about her failed exam. So when they asked how it went, she was able to tell them what I did and explain the gospel to them. She said their response was, "I wish I had your dad." Even that was a teaching moment as we talked about how we should be so joyful from God's grace that others would respond by saying, "I wish I had your God." Then I quickly reminded her that she had better start studying again. (I don't give my kids ice cream for every failing; this was a one-time lesson in grace. As fun as it was to thoroughly bless her when she deserved to face the consequences of her actions, we need to remember that "the Lord disciplines the one he loves" (Heb. 12:6).)

There's an old expression: most of what your kids learn from you will be caught, not taught. While it's not in the Bible, we all know there is a lot of truth in that statement. We can all think of habits, expressions, and attitudes that we picked up from our parents—for better or worse. They didn't sit us down and lecture us on these things, but we ended up copying them (many times even when we tried hard not to!).

Our kids have seen that we rarely live in our house by ourselves. We have constantly shared our home with others in need of a place to live. Some of those people have become our dearest friends. There were times when it was a major inconvenience, but we sought to be hospitable and love as Christ loved. There have even been times when the kids were in tears over some of our houseguests. We look back and laugh now, but it was tough on them at times. Those are good memories for them, to see that following Christ's example isn't always easy. Because of how frequently they experienced it growing up, I would be really surprised if my kids don't open their homes to those in need when they're living on their own.

Throughout our lives, we will continue to serve our children so that they can see an example of Christ. But we also need to teach them to serve others—they need to live Christ's example as well. Our job is not just to serve them, but to teach them to serve. Many think that parents should work hard to save for a comfortable retirement and to leave a large inheritance for their kids. But what if that impedes their growth as servants? No one wants to become a burden to others, but Scripture actually teaches that God likes seeing children care for their parents:

> If a widow has children or grandchildren, let them first learn to show godliness to their own household and to make some return to their parents, for this is pleasing in the sight of God... But if anyone does not provide for his relatives, and especially for members of his household, he has denied the faith and is worse than an unbeliever. (1 Timothy 5:4, 8)

Christian children should feel honored to be able to bless the parents who served them in their early years. Rather than seeing parents as a burden, God's design was for children to joyfully serve their parents. I expect my children to help care for me one day, if I live that long. Hopefully, I've raised grateful children who would count it an honor to take care of mom or dad one day.

PARENTING IN LIGHT OF GOD'S MISSION

I work a lot. And I definitely travel more than most. Hardly a week goes by where I'm not jumping on a plane, wishing I could just stay home with my family. Some would call this bad parenting. I would argue that. I don't neglect my children by any stretch of the imagination, but there are many times when I know God has called me to serve Him in ways that disrupt the family routine. I genuinely believe that it's good for my kids to observe this.

Following Jesus means that we put aside our personal desires and trust that the end result will be better. That's what Jesus meant when He said, "deny yourself, pick up your cross and follow me" (Luke 9:23). Good parenting means showing your children that the mission is bigger than any of us. Part of our mission is to develop a loving family that exemplifies relationships as they were meant to be, but the other part involves putting family aside when a greater mission calls (Matt. 10:37).

The kids need to see that I will miss some family dinners, piano recitals, and ball games when the mission demands it. This isn't a very popular idea in the American church, where we separate our love for God from our service to God. We say we love God most, but it's a vague statement that yields little action. Jesus spoke about more than feelings and emotions. He spoke of literal sacrifices that would disrupt our lives and possibly end them.

> As they were going along the road, someone said to him, "I will follow you wherever you go." And Jesus said to him, "Foxes have holes, and birds of the air have nests, but the Son of Man has nowhere to lay his head." To another he said, "Follow me." But he said, "Lord, let me first go and bury my father." And Jesus said to him, "Leave the dead to bury their own dead. But as for you, go and proclaim the kingdom of God." Yet another said, "I will follow you, Lord, but let me first say farewell to those at my home." Jesus said to him, "No one

who puts his hand to the plow and looks back is
fit for the kingdom of God." (Luke 9:57–62)

If I am in a third world country helping to find solutions to poverty and starvation, and my kids are home crying because they miss me, my wife quickly reminds them how blessed they are to have a dad who is out caring for others. If I'm out speaking and the kids are getting restless without me, she reminds them of the eternal significance. The moment I come home, I reassure them of how much I missed them and how I wish I could just stay with them all the time. And then I remind them again about the mission. As my kids have gotten older, I'll often take one of them along as I minister different places so that we can spend time pursuing the mission together.

It's healthy for my kids to give up their dad temporarily so that he can care for children who have no fathers. It teaches them how to sacrifice for those in need. It's important for them to understand that the mission involves saving people from eternal torment, so we must all be willing to make sacrifices for a greater purpose.

In fact, if they don't see the sacrifices made, they will later question whether or not we truly believe what we say we believe. They will eventually get to the age where they can reason logically and ask themselves why we spent so much time playing as a family when we knew that so many on earth were suffering, dying, and headed for hell. Maybe this is why 75 percent of church-raised children ditch the church when they turn 18. They see the gap between our supposed beliefs and our actions and decide not to join the hypocrisy.

My friends Brad and Beth Buser were missionaries in Papua New Guinea, living in a jungle with a tribe called the Iteri people. They spent 20 years trying to understand the Iteri language, sharing the gospel with them, putting the Iteri language into writing for the first time ever, teaching these people to read their own language, and creating an Iteri translation of the New Testament. Through this ministry, people were saved and a church was planted that lives on in their absence.

Brad and Beth raised four children in the jungles of Papua New Guinea. These kids witnessed the hardships their parents endured. Whether it was threats of violence (natives holding spears to their faces), severe sicknesses (once Brad was airlifted out in a coma), or just the day to day demands of ministry amongst an unreached people, they saw it all.

Brad tells me that one of the blessings of his life was sitting his kids down when they turned 18 and being able to say to them, "You saw that there was nothing mom and dad were not willing to sacrifice for the gospel, not even our lives. Now go and do the same." How many of us are living in such a way that we can say the same to our children?

It's hard to know which is the greater blessing: that the Iteri people are worshiping Jesus for the first time in history, or that all four of Brad and Beth's kids love Jesus and that the two oldest children are back in the jungles of Papua New Guinea reaching other lost tribes.

Make sure the mission of God is the priority in your life. Let your kids see, and give them opportunities to join you in serving

God. As they experience the joy of serving, the hope is that they will still be serving Him faithfully long after you are gone.

PARENTING IN LIGHT OF GOD'S PROMISES

Don't let a day go by without talking about heaven. The greatest lesson you can teach your kids is how to make decisions with an eternal mindset. This doesn't mean that we ignore the physical and temporary issues before us, but that we deal with them from an eternal perspective. Teach your children that life is short and uncertain, but our future is not. Every funeral they attend, every family member that passes, every pet that dies will only reinforce this truth. Too many parents try to shield their kids from reality. It is only a matter of time before they figure it out for themselves. Help them process reality from an early age, and teach them why it matters.

We let our children in on many of the decisions we make, and we explain why we make them. We let them know when our finances are being redirected because we want to invest in heaven (Matt. 6:19–20). Because we've been open about these things, our kids have had the blessing of seeing God come through for us in so many different ways. They see how God has been true to His promises in the smaller things, which gives them certainty about His promises of eternal riches.

Our kids are so certain and excited about heaven that they sometimes make statements that others find morbid. I remember being on a plane with the whole family when one of the kids said, "Dad, wouldn't it be cool if this plane crashed? Then we could all go to heaven together!" I agreed, but I'm sure the people around us thought we were pretty weird.

We have raised kids who aren't overly afraid of death. I also believe they are prepared for the time that mom and dad go to be with Jesus. While they will probably mourn as much as any other child would, Lisa and I are confident that they will trust in Christ rather than rebel against Him. We made sure they knew from the very beginning that life is short and unpredictable. We have always insisted that this is why we live for eternity and rejoice in God's promise for our future.

LOVE, FEAR, & SURRENDER —Lisa

It can be difficult to battle the desire to be our child's friend, rather than their authority.

I met once with a young married woman who did not have kids yet. Somehow we got on the topic of dating unbelievers, and I shared with her what we have always told our kids. If they are committed to following Jesus, we will not support them in a relationship with someone who is not following Jesus. She was shocked that we would hold to this standard at any age, with no exceptions. She was worried that holding kids to this standard would push them to rebel.

I'm going to be honest, I was pretty disheartened at this line of thinking. Should parents really make following Jesus more palatable to their kids so they won't find His commands so hard to deal with? I would argue that this actually sends a terrifying message to kids: you get to pick and choose which commands to follow and at which age.

The thing is, we have no guarantee that our children will not rebel. And chances are (being that they're sinners), they *will* rebel in some ways as they learn to live for God. But I certainly don't want to be the one who eases up on the standards or sugarcoats the rules in an effort to appease my kids. This would clearly show that I fear them more than I fear God. It's tempting to parent out of fear like that.

A few days after that lunch, I happened to read this passage:

> "Take to heart all the words by which I am warning you today, that you may command them to your children, that they may be careful to do all the words of this law. For it is no empty word for you, but your very life…" (Deuteronomy 32:46–47)

Are you willing to take a stand against your kids when God's Word is at stake? This doesn't mean you don't "speak the truth in love" and genuinely show your concern for their hearts. Ask yourself, what is truly the most loving thing I can do for them: Let them play around with God's laws? Or hold up God's laws as the standard by which we live? After all, these commands are *our very life.*

Remember the priest Eli in the book of Samuel? His story truly intrigues me. He himself had been a faithful priest, but it says his two older sons were "worthless men," and "did not know God," Eli heard about the evil things his sons were doing; taking meat from the offerings that didn't belong to them, taking things by force, and sleeping with women in the temple. It does say Eli rebuked them, which apparently meant telling them, "you guys shouldn't be doing these things!" But clearly God expected Eli to remove his sons from service and punish them for all they had done. His unwillingness to honor God led to severe judgment! Through Samuel, God revealed to Eli his punishment:

> On that day I will fulfill against Eli all that I have spoken concerning his house, from beginning to end. And I declare to him that I am about to punish his house forever, for the iniquity that he knew, because his sons were blaspheming God, and he did not restrain them. (1 Samuel 3:12–13)

> God also said earlier that Eli honored his sons above Him (2:29).

This is a heavy passage. But it's important for us to remember that our children should be expected to obey. Even at a young age we have to remind them that what God says, goes. There are plenty of Scriptures that show God's heart for obedience in our youth (e.g., Gen. 18:19; 1 Sam. 2:18–19, 26; Ps. 71:17; Luke 18:15–17; 1 Tim. 4:12).

Teenagers are not exempt from God's law. As they get older, they will struggle as they decide whether or not they themselves want to follow God. But we cannot back down from God's standards out of a fear of rebellion.

It breaks my heart to think of my children not walking with God. It would be almost unbearable. But the truth is, we are not the Holy Spirit. Only the Holy Spirit can enter our children's lives, make them new and different, and give them the desire to follow God. The truth is, somewhere in my heart is this hidden hope that maybe if I do everything "right," and share just the right Bible verses, and pray my knees off, they will be amazing Jesus-loving kids. There has to be a formula somewhere!

But there's not. And this is so very humbling. As parents, we absolutely need to pursue Christlikeness on our own. We should definitely share Bible verses with our kids. And our greatest weapon is certainly prayer. But we are not doing these things to save our children! Only God can do that.

We are doing these things so that our conscience can be at rest in Gods' presence. And we are doing them because we genuinely love our kids and want to give them as accurate a picture of loving Jesus as we can. When your kids are struggling or starting to stray, don't give up. Keep living out your faith. Don't let the enemy send you into despair with lies and hopelessness.

You are not perfect, and you never will be. We will all have failures as parents. The real question is: Is your life characterized by a pursuit of Christ? If it is, then you can humbly accept your mistakes without being crippled. If it is not, then you can repent and believe that God can transform not only your life, but the lives of your children too.

Maybe you getting serious about your walk with God will be just the thing He uses to turn them back to Him. Wouldn't that be incredible?

Recently, a younger couple asked us how to have a close relationship with their kids. The wife explained to us, "I didn't share *anything* with my parents." Just the fact that she wanted a different type of relationship with her kids was a step in the right direction.

Answering this question led me to a realization: One of the best ways to connect with your children is to be connected with your spouse. So much of a child's security comes from trusting that mom and dad are a strong unit. Think about it. If you are teaching your kids what it means to follow Christ, and you and your spouse are living that out in your home, it will make sense to them. They will be drawn to you and the fruit of the Spirit that comes from your life.

Your integrity in marriage will have a huge impact on your children. This does not mean that they will not see you work through conflict or have bad days here and there. But your kids need to know that you're the real deal. It's not enough to wake up early on Sundays, throw your kids in the car, fight all the way to church, and then go about your own business the rest of the week. As important as a commitment to the church is, your kids need to see God's truth shaping your lives throughout the week. If they can see you living out the gospel in the most intimate relationship you have, they will have an authentic picture of what it means to live according to the *Word* rather than the *world*.

It matters how you treat your spouse in front of your children. It's extremely important how you talk about your spouse when he is not there. Your kids are not dummies. They pick up on disrespect, irritation, and lack of love. But they also pick up on grace, patience, and a loving attitude. What message are you sending to your children? Do they see you taking the Word of God seriously?

We can't be Christians who "just don't love our spouses." It doesn't work like that. After Christ, the relationship you have with your husband or wife is *the* most influential relationship you have. So many kids are derailed from their faith as they watch their believing parents fail to love one another well. I'm talking about believing parents—parents in whom the Holy Spirit is supposed to be living.

Yes, there are other things that will tempt your kids, and other reasons they may choose not to follow Christ. But do you really want to add another potential stumbling block to your kids' faith simply because you don't "feel like" loving your husband or wife? Paul says, "*so far as it depends on you*, live peaceably with all" (Rom. 12:18). Do what it takes, by the power of the Spirit, to live out the gospel in your marriage relationship. There is so much at stake.

LOVE

Everyone says, "Don't sweat the small stuff." That is especially true in parenting. I was praying for my son the other day, getting caught up in some small worries, when I suddenly cut to the chase. My strongest desire for my son is that he would be a man of integrity, that his character would outshine any other thing in his life. So I stopped praying about the minor issues and started begging God to make my son into a man of integrity. Keeping my prayers focused on the big picture helps me not to get off track. It also keeps me from being disheartened when things are difficult.

Our kids hear us pray often that we would all love God more and more. Truly, that is the heart behind every prayer we will ever pray for them. To love God more is the fulfillment of the Great Commandment (Mark 12:28–30). It's the one thing that will keep them in step with His Spirit and obeying His word. We don't want kids that are "religious" and shy away from cussing or watching

R-rated movies. We want kids that love God with their whole heart, and live their lives to please Him.

FEAR

Parenting can be full of fears. I bought a plaque the other day for my home that says, "Let your faith be bigger than your fear." What a great reminder to have in front of me every day. I desperately need my faith to be bigger than my fear! I wish I was naturally fearless and courageous and bold. But I'm not. It is a constant battle for me.

My struggle with fear was amplified when I became a mom. Suddenly the desire for safety and comfort threatened to swallow up my desire to follow Christ at any cost. In parenting, it's very important to remember who <u>you</u> belong to, not just who your children belong to. You are not your own, you were bought with a price (1 Cor. 6:19–20). Jesus says:

> If anyone comes to me and does not hate his own father and mother and wife and children and brothers and sisters, yes, and even his own life, he cannot be my disciple. Whoever does not bear his own cross and come after me cannot be my disciple. (Luke 14: 26–27)

That giant, all encompassing love we feel for our children should be lost and swallowed up in our love for Jesus.

Kids bring out the protector in us—that overwhelming desire to shield them from hurt and pain. But we have *no idea* what

God's plans are for our children. We do know, however, that His plans will certainly include struggles, trials, and heartache along their journey toward becoming godly men and women (2 Tim. 3:12, John 16:33). We have to stop being so fearful about everything and start trusting that God knows what He is doing.

When one of our daughters was 15, she had the opportunity to spend six weeks at an orphanage in Thailand. We had spent time at this orphanage as a family the year before, so she was dying to go back and see the children. The only problem was that she would need to make the international flight by herself, with a short layover in Japan. In my heart, I knew she should go. But in my fear, I wanted to keep her home! Honestly, I kept thinking about standing in the way of what God wanted to do, and I couldn't let that happen.

As we prayed about it, both Francis and I believed the Spirit was leading us to let her go. Some people thought we were a little crazy. Maybe they still do! But we believed that this was what God wanted, so we had to trust Him. We knew who would be on the other side of the world to pick her up in Thailand, and bring her safely to the orphanage. But much more importantly, we knew the One who would be with her at every moment, leading and guiding her through every circumstance. This was a precious opportunity for her to build her own faith and experience relying on God.

It isn't easy to let our children go. I cried my eyes out when her plane took off! But God reminded me that this is what it looked like in that moment to love *Him* most, to love Him so much I would willingly place my precious child into His care.

SURRENDER

If I had to say what scares me the most, I would definitely say that it's the thought of being tortured, or worse: watching my children taken and tortured or violated. I can't think of a more horrible thing. Many of us get stuck here, paralyzed by our "ultimate" fear. We get so caught up in our big, crazy fears that we fail to realize how much we resist surrendering in the "smaller" fears. It's this lack of surrender in our *everyday* lives that wreaks havoc in our walk with God.

Ultimately, the fear that stands most in my way is the fear of not being in control. I want things to go *my* way. I want to keep everyone happy and comfortable *my* way. But surrender is all about giving up control. It's inherently selfless. We struggle with fear and hesitate to surrender because it demands that we let go of ourselves and the ones we love. If you're a control freak, this is going to require serious prayer!

It can be devastating to realize that we don't even *want* to surrender in the everyday moments with God. But it's only devastating if you realize it and don't do anything about it. Challenge your heart on this. Do you have any intention or desire to surrender to God's will for your life, your marriage, or your kids? Because really, what good is a "believer" who doesn't trust God? What good is a "follower" of Christ who doesn't follow Christ? God calls us to surrender everything to Him. If we can't—or won't—there's no point in moving on from there. But if you want to—if you will—there's no better place to start.

CONCLUSION: THINK ABOUT THEIR FUTURE

It certainly doesn't appear that our children will have it easier than we did. On the contrary, it seems like they will live in a world that is more hostile towards biblical morality and God's sovereignty. The bullying has begun, and physical persecution seems imminent. Following Jesus around America will be more difficult for this generation. It will require greater strength. We need a generation of parents who care far more about the strength of their children than their comfort, wealth, health, and love for their parents.

James 1 tells us that strength is developed through trials. The way we learn to persevere is through actual testing. This is going to sound evil to some of you, but I (Francis) have actually prayed that my children would go through trials. If trials are the channel through which strength comes, wouldn't we want some trials?

Easy circumstances do not cultivate strong children. I want my kids to be strong because I have watched weak people cower when pressure came. I think the future is going to be difficult, and I want my kids to persevere. I want them to go through some trials while they are still under my care so I can shepherd them through it. I want to raise strong children.

We also want to raise kids whose lives revolve around God and His mission. So much of the advice you'll receive about parenting these days focuses on nourishing your children, caring for them, supporting them, helping them, etc. And that's great. But not if we're doing these things in such a way that our children become the center of our universe or the center of theirs.

Truly nourishing our children means teaching them to thrive in the real world. And here is the truest reality—God tells us that "from him and through him and to him are all things" (Rom. 11:36). God is at the center of the universe. He made this world to declare His glory. So we are not doing our kids any favors by lying to them about the nature of the universe. It's not about them: it's about Him.

Nor is the universe about us as parents. Our parenting must stand on the foundation of God's grace. Everything we do as parents must be focused on God, His glory, and His mission. Jesus' mission for His church is clear: "Go therefore and make disciples of all nations" (Matt. 28:18). Obviously this is much broader than parenting. But our parenting is not exempt from the command to make disciples. God has entrusted you with your children so that you would make them into disciples who will go into every part of the world and make disciples. This mission is too important to squander because of our insecurities, our longing for comfort, or our fears.

DO SOMETHING

If you are currently a parent, you will automatically be responding to this chapter in practical ways. The decisions you make in parenting will quickly reveal whether or not you're pursuing God and His mission in how you raise your children. But it's important to think this through, so use the following suggestions to assess your approach to parenting.

TALK WITH YOUR SPOUSE.

+ *For most of this book, you've been evaluating your relation-ship with your spouse. Now take a minute to have an honest conversation about your parenting. (If you don't yet have kids, you can choose which of these questions are appropriate and discuss them in terms of what you'd like to do in the future.)*

+ *What would you say has been your highest goal in parenting?*

+ *What would you say has been your greatest shortcoming in parenting?*

+ *Do you think your kids see themselves as the center of their own universe? Why do you say that?*

+ *What are some practical ways that you can begin to help them see God and His truth more clearly?*

+ *Are there any ways in which your relationship with each other needs to change so that your kids get a more accurate picture of God and His will?*

TALK WITH YOUR KIDS.

+ *If your children are old enough to have this type of conversa-tion, consider sitting down with them and asking them some important questions that relate to your parenting. Use these questions as teaching opportunities where you feel it is appro-priate or helpful.*

- *Ask your kids to be honest about their relationship with God. Make sure you allow them freedom to answer honestly. They will probably be tempted to just tell you what you want to hear. Tell them of your struggles to believe at their age, as that might give them permission to share their doubts and struggles. Do all you can to open the door for their honesty.*

- *Ask your kids how you can be praying for them as they fight to live holy lives and have influence on their campus. Pray specifically for some of their friends, then check back with them occasionally to see if God has answered these requests.*

- *Find out about their dreams. Ask them what they think their lives would look like in ten years if everything went according to their ideal plans.*

- *Talk with your spouse about the way your children answered. Is there anything you ought to change in the way you parent or with regard to your relationship with each other based on the way your children answered?*

The Amazing Race

CONCLUSION

Have you ever watched the reality show *The Amazing Race*? Contestants pair up to compete, and are given tasks and clues that lead them on a race all around the world. Couples are disqualified at the various checkpoints if they are too slow. The first couple to finish the entire journey wins the prize. I've only seen this show a few times, but I was entertained as I watched couples fight, waste precious time, and eventually lose. It was also inspiring (I'm sure the theme music helped), to watch couples encourage each other, work through challenges, and use each other's strengths to make it to the finish line.

At a recent marriage retreat, Lisa talked about how she saw our marriage like a long episode of *The Amazing Race*. The reason we don't often fight is because we don't have time to fight. We are busy trying to get to the finish line. Even in our victories, we only

184 you and me FOREVER

have time for short celebrations because time is ticking. A quick high-five and then it's on to the next checkpoint. We may take breaks to catch our breath, but we quickly get back in the race. Similar to Paul (1 Cor. 9:24-27), we view our life on earth as a race.

I was told by a marathon runner that you should try to run the second half of the race faster than the first. And once the finish line is in sight, many runners sprint. They use up every ounce of energy they have left because they know they can collapse once they break the tape.

I want to run my life in that same manner. I want the second half to be stronger than the first. In America, the norm is to do the opposite: do radical things for Christ when you are 18–25, then slow down once you are married. When you have children, your service to Jesus slows to a crawl—you have your family to think about. Then it's only a matter of time before you forget you are even in a race. Instead, you focus on building a home and settling down.

But it doesn't have to be this way. We can run faster as the race goes on. In our final years, we can sprint, knowing that we can collapse into His arms.

LEARN FROM THE ELDERLY

Joshua and Caleb are great examples for us. In their early years, they were the only two spies who had faith in God's ability to lead them to victory. Caleb recounts the story in his later years in Joshua 14 (it's definitely worth the read). He tells of the early days when everyone doubted, but he and Joshua were ready to fight. Therefore, God declared that only Joshua and Caleb would enter the Promised Land. Everyone else would die in the desert. The most inspiring part of his speech is the end:

> "And now, behold, the LORD has kept me alive, just as he said, these forty-five years since the time that the LORD spoke this word to Moses, while Israel walked in the wilderness. And now, behold, I am this day eighty-five years old. I am still as strong today as I was in the day that Moses sent me; my strength now is as my strength was then, for war and for going and coming. So now give me this hill country of which the LORD spoke on that day, for you heard on that day how the Anakim were there, with great fortified cities. It may be that the LORD will be with me, and I shall drive them out just as the LORD said." (Joshua 14:10–12)

At 85, Caleb was as courageous as ever. Rarely do we meet people in their fifties and sixties living by faith, much less people in their eighties. In speaking to young adults throughout America, they tell me of how they would love to be mentored by older people who are living by faith. But they can't find any. Some may be joyful and friendly, but no longer living by faith. Sadly, their lives consist of visiting grandkids and taking vacations. Some are still acquiring more possessions, hoping to make the most of their last few days on earth.

This is the opposite of Caleb. At 85, the end was in sight. He was sprinting for the finish line. He experienced the faithfulness of God throughout his lifetime, and it only made him more courageous as life went on.

Then there's Joshua, who spoke these words at the end of his life:

> "And now I am about to go the way of all the earth, and you know in your hearts and souls, all of you, that not one word has failed of all the good things that the LORD your God promised concerning you. All have come to pass for you; not one of them has failed." (Joshua 23:14)

That's the kind of speech I want to give at the end of my life. Don't you? Don't you want to be able to look at your loved ones and tell them about how faithful God was during your lifetime? And don't you want to encourage them to follow your example in staying faithful to the God who was so faithful to His promises?

Joshua and Caleb started well and finished well. They were faithful to the end and entered the Promised Land. The Bible doesn't say much about the relationship between Joshua and Caleb, but try to imagine the bond they must have had. They were the only two who believed, and they never stopped believing. No one on earth experienced the goodness of God like they did. Now in their final days, they recount stories of God's trustworthiness to the next generation.

If the Lord wills that Lisa and I live that long, I pray we would also have that kind of camaraderie. I pray that we would be able to look back at a lifetime of adventure and tell the next generation to follow our example.

Not everyone finishes well. Few do. A friend of mine recently left his wife for another woman. What baffles me is that he is in his late sixties and has been in ministry for over 40 years. Really? You're inches from the finish line and you decided to stop and run the other direction? Satan is alive and well for now. Don't be unaware of his schemes. I have seen old men and old women make stupid choices at the end of their lives. For those who are reading this in their latter years: don't be stupid. Sprint for the finish line. Finish strong.

SOME THINGS ARE WORTH THE WAIT

I can't wait for heaven.

And that's one of my biggest problems. There are days when I don't want to wait any longer. I want comfort now, riches now, rewards now.

We are part of the most impatient generation in history. We are so accustomed to getting things immediately that sometimes waiting 10 or 20 seconds makes us angry. This is a real problem because God has called us to be good at waiting. Christians should be diligently waiting (Matt 25). Hebrews tells us that Christ is coming back to save "those who are eagerly waiting for him" (9:28). But in reality, we are terrible at waiting.

It baffles us that the Israelites couldn't even wait for Moses to come down from the mountain. We think it's ridiculous that they became so impatient that they gathered gold and created an idol to worship (Ex. 32). It was a stupid and costly mistake, but many of us do the same thing! We can't wait until Christ returns, so we gather up our riches to set up a counterfeit paradise. We try to isolate our family in a safe community and provide ourselves with whatever our hearts desire. We try to create our own heaven on earth.

Many choose to become Christians because they think it will make life easier. Jesus warned that it would actually make life far more difficult (Luke 14:25-35). Paul promised the same: "Indeed, all who desire to live a godly life in Christ Jesus will be persecuted" (2 Tim. 3:12). God has called us to far more than attending church services and raising nice children. We are in a race, a fight, a war. Those who decide to follow Jesus have signed themselves up for a life of suffering. The solution is not to dodge trials but to persevere through them.

But we can use the pain to our advantage. It can remind us that "this light momentary affliction is preparing for us an eternal weight of glory beyond all comparison" (2 Cor. 4:17). The pain in life can remind us of future rewards. Each time we suffer, we can praise God for His promise of a better future. For now, we wait with the rest of creation.

CROSSING THE FINISH LINE

Wherever you are in the journey, picture how you want this life to end. We make our best decisions in hindsight, so imagine yourself standing before God. How would your ideal life have looked?

For me, I hope I will have lived a life full of faith and sacrifice for His Kingdom. I hope I will have grown in faith and courage every year. It would be great to know that I graciously endured suffering and rejection for His sake during my time on earth. I certainly don't want to stand before Him having lived a cowardly life. I want to be one of those who comes out of the war with scars—just like Jesus.

Seriously consider how you want to approach the throne. Is your life currently on the right trajectory? Or do you need to make changes? Don't get overwhelmed by how much time you have already wasted, and don't dwell too long on past mistakes. Just take the next step. And keep the end in view.

For Lisa and I, writing this book was our next step of obedience. We hope to bring some change to the way couples view life. We want to be faithful to getting this message to as many people as possible. That's why we made it free for people to read and pass on. If you know of a couple who needs the message of this book, let them know that they can download it for free at www.youandmeforever.org.

I can't tell you what God wants you to do next. It would be wise for you and your spouse to spend extended periods of time in prayer. Ask God to guide you wherever He wants to lead. If you are still stuck, start wherever you are.

In Acts 1:8, Jesus told His followers that the Spirit would empower them to be His witness "in Jerusalem and in all Judea and Samaria, and to the end of the earth." Of course, God was doing something unique through those original disciples. But it's significant that His plan for them started in their own neighborhood—Jerusalem—and then spread out from there. This may be an uncomfortable first step for you, but consider taking walks around your neighborhood together. Pray for each house as you pass. I think you'll be surprised at the outcome as you pray in faith. Ask Him for opportunities to share the gospel, and take the opportunities He provides.

Time flies. And it flies faster each year. So don't procrastinate. Think of your age in miles per hour. When you're seven years old, it feels like life is moving at seven miles per hour. It feels like you are never going to turn eight. When you're in your twenties and thirties, the years start passing by more rapidly. By the time you're doing fifty or sixty, it's hard to even keep track of what year it is. Anything beyond that, and you're in the fast lane. You should just put this book down now and sprint. Like a game of hot potato, you should get rid of your possessions as fast as possible. Invest everything you can in the Kingdom. Your life is going to be over any minute, and you're going to regret holding on to things you weren't able to keep.

THE END

You usually want to end a book with your strongest point so it lingers in the reader's mind. We believe the most powerful thing we can end with is prayer. So here is our prayer for our marriage and for yours. We strongly encourage you to pray this together:

> *God, help us love You deeply and fear You greatly.*
> *Teach us how to love each other for Your sake.*
> *May the humility of Christ be seen in the way we*
>   *treat each other.*

Show us how to enjoy each other without neglecting
     Your mission.
Remind us of the brevity of life so we share
     Your good news urgently.
Remind us of heaven so we will face rejection
     and trials joyfully.
When we settle down for too long, prod us to run.
When we are prone to fight, teach us to fight
     together, and to fight for You.
When we are tempted to run away, bring repen-
     tance and renewal.
May we spend our married days reminding each
     other of Your glory, Your gospel, Your love,
     Your power, Your mission, and Your promise
     of what is to come.
Amen.

NOTES

1. A. W. Tozer, *The Knowledge of the Holy* (San Francisco: Harper-San Francisco, 1992), 3.

2. Recorded in Erwin W. Lutzer, *When a Nation Forgets God: 7 Lessons We Must Learn from Nazi Germany* (Chicago: Moody Publishers, 2010), 21–22.